THE
MARX BROTHERS

THE MARX BROTHERS

A Pyramid Illustrated History of the Movies

by
WILLIAM WOLF

Research Associate: **LILLIAN KRAMER WOLF**

General Editor: **TED SENNETT**

PYRAMID
PUBLICATIONS
NEW YORK

To my mother
Charlotte Wolf Jacobs

THE MARX BROTHERS
A Pyramid Illustrated History of the Movies

Copyright © 1975 by Pyramid Communications, Inc.

Pyramid edition published October 1975

ISBN 0-515-03754-0

Library of Congress Catalog Card Number: 75-29948

Printed in the United States of America

Pyramid Books are published by Pyramid Communications, Inc. Its trademarks, consisting of the word "Pyramid" and the portrayal of a pyramid, are registered in the United States Patent Office.

Pyramid Communications, Inc., 919 Third Avenue, New York, N.Y. 10022

(graphic design by ANTHONY BASILE)

ACKNOWLEDGMENTS

To the staff and facilities of the Lincoln Center Library of the Performing Arts, Theatre Collection, and similar appreciation for the facilities of the main branch of the New York Public Library. To Ted Sennett for his astute editorial guidance and assistance. To my wife Lillian, for her diligent research. To the Marx Brothers for some of the most wonderful hours I have ever spent.

Photographs: Jerry Vermilye, The Memory Shop, Cinemabilia, Gene Andrewski, Movie Star News, Quality First, United Press International, the Lincoln Center of the Performing Arts, and the companies that produced and distributed the films of the Marx Brothers: Paramount Pictures Corp., Metro-Goldwyn-Mayer, Inc., RKO Radio Pictures, David L. Loew Productions, Lester Cowan Productions, Warner Brothers, Inc., and United Artists.

Passages from *Harpo Speaks!* are quoted with the permission of Freeway Press.

CONTENTS

Introduction 11

How They Got That Way 15

Rehearsal for the Movies 27

Paramount Years 39

Roaring with the Lion 77

Onward and Downward 95

Immortality 132

Bibliography 147

The Major Films of the Marx Brothers 149

Miscellany 152

Index 155

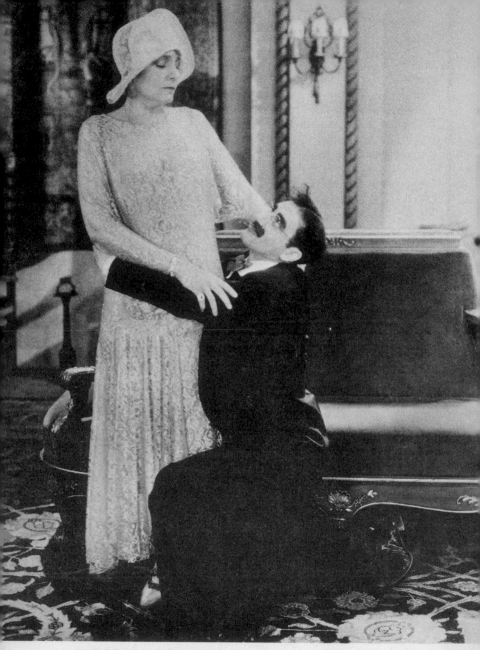

THE COCOANUTS (1929). Groucho courts Margaret Dumont.

INTRODUCTION

A loud cheer thundered through the Palais du Festival at the Cannes International Film Festival on the evening of May 14, 1972, as Groucho Marx walked slowly on stage, led by his attractive companion, Erin Fleming. Waiting to honor Groucho with the Commandeur des Arts et Lettres award in tribute to the legendary Marx Brothers films stood Robert Favre-Le Bret, the festival director. Groucho moved feebly, his eyes twinkling, but at the age of eighty-one a shadow of the man who had just been cavorting on screen in the hilarious *A Night at the Opera*.

The classic comedy shown to the international audience had French subtitles. Imagine a bewildered linguist with the perplexing task of translating Marxian madness into French. Through stretches of the picture, the subtitler apparently just gave up. Foreign subtitles couldn't adequately convey the inspired, idiomatic nonsense. Efforts to do so were sometimes funny in themselves, as in the famous scene of Groucho and Chico decimating a legal contract, tearing away pieces that they determine are not needed.

Chico questions a portion of the proposed agreement. Groucho: "It's all right. That's—that's in every contract. That's—that's what they call a sanity clause." Chico: "You can't fool me. There ain't no Sanity Claus." The subtitle read:

"C'est la clause sanitaire." ("It's the sanitary clause.")

It was a hopeless pun for translation. But the audience laughed anyway, and at just about everything else in the picture. Now, thirty-seven years after the film was released, it was delighting a sophisticated festival audience as it had delighted millions through several generations. The Marx brothers are hardly subject to such trivialities as language barriers.

Groucho quickly took command on stage and gave his audience a sample of the type of comedy for which he was famous. He listened with a dubious expression on his face while austere-looking Favre-Le Bret read the citation. For a moment they seemed to be re-enacting the contract scene just witnessed in the film, and one expected Groucho to tear off a strip of the text. The director solemnly completed his pronouncement, draped a medal around Groucho's neck, and like Margaret Dumont waiting for the next line, paused.

Groucho, glancing teasingly at Favre-Le Bret, summoned his best French to respond: "Voulez-vous coucher avec moi?" Said the taken-aback official: "I'll have to think about it." Groucho then went on to thank the festival and note seriously that he wished Harpo and Chico could have been alive to share in the honor. Whereupon, not overlooking the dirty-old-man role he had been acting through most of his career, he introduced Miss Fleming over and over again.

"I'd like you to meet my (leer) secretary . . . This (leer) is my secretary . . . "Erin (leer), would you come out here again . . . . Folks, this is my secretary."

For all the merriment, there was a sadness to the event. Here in 1972, Groucho was so feeble that he had to be helped wherever he walked. Chico and Harpo were gone. It had taken a long time for the most celebrated of international film festivals to pay homage to Groucho, as it had done belatedly the year before to Charlie Chaplin. Groucho was nonetheless delighted by it all and made the most of the situation. He was *the* celebrity of the moment at Cannes. Journalists, critics, and admirers were passing up current stars and starlets for a chance to follow Groucho around as he made the scene.

Typical was an intimate luncheon for a few critics at the prestigious Le Moulin restaurant in nearby Mougins. Groucho and Gina Lollobrigida were the honored guests. Everyone had to strain to hear the repartée, on the quiet side because Groucho's voice was so frail.

"Hello, Gina, what do you hear from the Pope?" was Groucho's greeting. She seemed flustered at being put in the position of playing straight-woman to the mischief-maker across the table.

"Are you married, Gina?"

"Not at the moment."

"Well, the Pope isn't married either," came the typical non sequitur. Then Gina got in a few quips of her own. If she minded that the attention was being focused on Groucho, she didn't betray it. The scene was similar everywhere Groucho went. Despite his weak physical state, he enjoyed making people strain to catch each of his one-liners and anecdotes about the past.

The pleasure of being "rediscovered" in the waning years of one's life is rare. It happened to Buster Keaton shortly before he died. Chaplin was invited back to Hollywood in the movie industry's effort to atone for his exile during the McCarthy years. The Marx Brothers revival brought Groucho into the limelight for one more symbolic "hurrah." Later, when *Animal Crackers* reopened in New York in June, 1974, at the Sutton Theater, after not having been shown for two decades as a result of entanglements over rights, Groucho was on hand for the occasion, which was treated as a premiere. Mounted police were needed to help contain the mob of fans, most of them young, eager for a look at the man

A DAY AT THE RACES (1937). The Marxes and Esther Muir

who made them laugh so hard and so often.

When Groucho went to the fashionable "21" restaurant for a party in his honor, he involved waiters and patrons in his hi-jinks. He was handed a tie and told to put it on in order to be admitted. Later he asked waiters and diners alike to take off their ties in a show of solidarity. He also had the waiters lifting up their trousers in response to his question: "Have you got frog's legs?"

Animal Crackers was only one of the Marx Brothers film revivals. Their pictures are continually turning up on double bills, or in retrospectives. Youngsters are taken to them by parents who are eager to introduce them to Marxian mayhem. (My younger daughter, Karen, an early film fan, would repeatedly say, even before she could remember their name, "Is anything playing with those brothers?") Their films continue to generate the kind of bellylaughs few others can equal.

Where did these marvelous Marxes come from? How did they get started? What was it like making their films? What are some of the memorable highlights of their films? Did they realize their full potential? Why did their films decline in comic quality?

Ultimately we also face the intriguing question: Why have the Marx Brothers films persisted through the years as comedy classics, reaching across to new generations and transcending international boundaries?

Stage mothers have taken a hard rap in the lore of show business. They are the butt of jokes, most of them deserved, and many a producer or theatrical manager has run for cover at the sight of a traditional stage mother invading the premises to browbeat, cajole, or salespitch her offspring into an opportunity to face an audience. Minnie Marx certainly was not short on qualities associated with stage motherhood. The difference was that three of the sons she was grooming and pushing into the limelight had monumental comic talent.

All Marx Brothers enthusiasts owe a debt of gratitude to Minnie. Without her diligence and determination, her ingenuity and love of show business, her sons would never have reached their phenomenal success. They probably would not even have been in show business at all. It was Minnie who conceived of their careers, shaped their early performing, and maneuvered with all her tenacious skills to get them bookings.

Alexander Woollcott, the eminent critic who played such an important role in acclaiming the Marxes as big-time stars when their first Broadway show opened, wrote in *The New Yorker* of September 28, 1929, upon Minnie's death following a stroke: "She had done much more than bear her sons, bring them up, and turn them into

HOW THEY GOT THAT WAY

play actors. She had invented them. They were just comics she imagined for her own amusement. They amused no one more, and their reward was her ravishing smile."

Harpo, writing of his mother in his autobiography, *Harpo Speaks!* says: "She was a lovely woman, but her soft, doelike looks were deceiving. She had the stamina of a brewery horse, the drive of a salmon fighting his way up a waterfall, the cunning of a fox, and a devotion to her brood as fierce as any she-lion's . . .

"Minnie's plan was simply this: to put her kid brother and her five sons on the stage and make them successful. She went to work down the line starting with Uncle Al (who'd changed his name from Schoenberg to Shean), then took up, in order, Groucho, Gummo, myself, Chico and Zeppo. This was one hell of a job. What made it even tougher was the fact that only Uncle Al and Groucho wanted to be in show business in the first place, and after Groucho got a taste of the stage, he wanted to be a writer. Chico wanted to be a professional gambler. Gummo wanted to be an inventor. Zeppo wanted to be a prize fighter. I wanted to play the piano on a ferryboat."*

The hectic, economically difficult life of the Marx family was similar to that of other Jewish families struggling for survival at a time when immigrants to America were hoping to provide their children with a brighter future. New York's Lower East Side was the classic launching pad of numerous show business careers, but the Upper East Side was the stomping ground of the Marx Brothers. The ethnic mixture in the neighborhood at the time, the latter part of the nineteenth century and the beginning of the twentieth, was primarily German and Irish, and the boys, while growing up, had their share of battles that went along with being Jewish kids in that corner of New York's melting pot. Though the family moved many times, the one address that became home for a substantial period was a tenement at 179 East 93rd Street.

The family's relationship with show business dated back to the Marx Brothers' grandparents on Minnie's side. Lafe and Fanny Schoenberg were performers in Germany before coming to America. Lafe worked as a magician and ventriloquist, and Fanny was a yodelling harpist. But their stage prospects proved to be bleak in America and Lafe took to fixing umbrellas. Groucho says that judging by the number of umbrellas he actually repaired, "it must have been the driest season in the New York weather bureau." Fanny died shortly after the family moved to 93rd Street; Lafe lived to be one hundred and one. Groucho recalls his grandfather smoking ten cigars a day made from leaves rejected by a tobacco factory, and when not puffing away at the cigars, nursing a pipe that "could give any skunk a lesson in pungency."

Minnie was fifteen years old by the time her parents came to America, and she went to work in a factory making straw hats. Sam Marx, who was from the Alsace, emigrated for the same reason that brought many other young men here: to avoid being drafted. In New York he worked as an instructor in a dance school. Sam, nicknamed "Frenchie," became a tailor. Groucho says his father, called "misfit Sam," was a better cook than a tailor. Frenchie hated to use a tape measure, and, says Groucho, "never had the same customer twice."

Frenchie and Minnie met at the dance school. She was eighteen when they were married. The future stars arrived in this order:

Chico (Leonard), March 22, 1887; Harpo (Adolph, later known as Arthur), November 23, 1888; Groucho (Julius Henry), October 2, 1890, with Gummo (Milton)

*Harpo Marx, *Harpo Speaks!*, Freeway Press, New York, 1974, pp. 23-24.

16

Minnie Marx, mother of the Marx Brothers

joining the family in 1897, and Zeppo (Herbert) in 1901.

The formative years of the Marxes are especially important in relation to their films. Not only do they lead to the career path that, in turn, led to films, but the character types that were the mainstays of their pictures took shape in their environment long before they performed. The lineage of the comic characteristics of Chico, Harpo, and Groucho can be traced clearly and directly. Even allowing for the embellishment that goes with reminiscences of childhood and for the ways of publicity aimed at maintaining a public image, the Marx brothers appear to have slipped into stage clowning based on their real-life exploits and personalities.

Their youth was characterized by a daily hustle to keep one step ahead of economic disaster, and the brothers operated in that atmosphere just as frantically as they hustled in *Room Service*. Crucially, the element of humor was also present, with mother Minnie being the centrifugal force. Harpo recalled: "It was Minnie who kept our lives full of laughter. . . . We were like a family of castaways surviving on a desert island. . . . It was us against the elements, and each of us found his own way to survive. Frenchie took to tailoring; Chico to the poolroom; I took to the streets; Minnie held us all together while she plotted our rescue."[*]

A film script could be developed from the early bouts with the landlord and the frenzied maneuvers to keep poverty away from the door. Chico was the major family wheeler-dealer, and nothing said by his brothers in recounting their early years indicates that he had many scruples about doing what suited him at the moment. When something was missing in the apartment, the pall of suspicion would quickly settle upon Chico, who most likely had pawned the item. Things were missing often. Groucho speaks of his father's tailoring shears, and of his grandfather's walking cane with an impressive silver head.

Chico had a special talent for mathematics, which he deftly parlayed into enhancing his ability at gambling and card playing. He also haunted the pool halls, bet on horses and boxing matches, and he shot craps regularly. Gambling became a compulsion which stayed with Chico throughout his life, much to the chagrin of his brothers, who tried to keep him from squandering the money he earned during the successful years.

Chico also knew the ropes, and as a kid in the neighborhood honed his talent for making contacts, going where the action was, and always trying to gratify his desperate need for gambling money. He

[*]*Harpo Speaks!*, p. 24.

was also the Marx brother most successful with the girls, and his brothers envied him for this.

Meanwhile, Chico was learning to play the piano at twenty-five cents a lesson as Minnie began to nurture the idea of turning her boys into stage material. Even the twenty-five cents was a sacrifice in the Marx household. Chico was supposed to repeat each lesson he took for Harpo, but he was too busy with his assorted activities, and Harpo had to fend for himself on the piano that his mother bought.

Harpo wrote in his autobiography that Chico's teacher only knew how to play with his right hand and faked the left, and that's why Chico became the best one-handed piano player in the neighborhood. The story may be far-fetched, but it can be said that Chico, through those early lessons, was preparing for those marvelous piano romps that became a staple in Marx Brothers films. Chico also exhibited an early talent for doing accents, Italian being the one that stuck for his performing. But he could also do Irish, German, and Jewish accents.

Harpo, who looked a lot like Chico, left school in his second bout with second grade. The other kids used to tease and bully him, and one boy liked to drop Harpo out of the school's first floor window, an eight-foot fall. Dropped once too

often, he decided not to return. Harpo learned to develop his own resources, and he tried to ape Chico, who passed on his worldly knowledge about gambling, pool, and the need to hustle money, instead of relying on such conventional methods as a job.

An episode involving cuckoo clocks might have been born in a Marx Brothers film. Chico and Harpo began buying up miniature cuckoo clocks cheaply, and then resold them for a profit. Overzealous, Harpo promised one neighborhood businessman that a clock would run for eight hours on one winding. When the prospect promised to buy it if this were true, Harpo stood in the office sweating out the time, surreptitiously giving the chain short pulls when the customer had his back turned. When Harpo was caught, he fled. The money made on their clock gambit was dropped by Chico in a card game.

Harpo learned to live by his wits. He would scrounge for items he could sell to junk dealers, or hang around the tennis courts in the hope of getting a stray ball. Or he would hop trolley cars and play hide-and-seek with the conductor. For recreation he would swim in the garbage-strewn East River. There were often scrapes with the cops, but an uncle who was a Tammany Hall wheel stood ready to get him out of trouble. From Harpo's description of his youthful es-

The Marx family before World War I.
Left to right: Harpo, Chico, Samuel Marx,
Zeppo, Minnie Marx, Gummo, and Groucho

capades, it is but a short leap to the image of his outwitting cops in his films, or resembling a walking department store with loot concealed in his oversized coat.

Those marvelously wacky faces he is famous for on screen also had their early origin. Harpo was enthralled by the humorous appearance of a man known as Gookie, who rolled cigars in a store window. Harpo learned to do an exaggerated imitation of Gookie, and would amuse everyone in the neighborhood with the caricature. Harpo found that he could get a laugh whenever he would "throw a Gookie," and that routine continued through his show business career. Harpo later enlarged upon his comic propensities by having fun with a blond wig he borrowed from Groucho when his brother was a delivery boy for a wig company. He would put on his mother's clothes and in that get-up, play practical jokes.

Meanwhile, Harpo was also exhibiting the sensitivity that became the other side of the coin in his film routines. He was considered the particularly kind, solid member of the family. He was also somewhat of a loner, lost in his own private world of thoughts. His fascination with the harp began with an old harp that had belonged to his grandmother.

Harpo suffered through a variety of jobs. He worked for a time as a pie sorter, and as a butcher shop delivery boy, but he was fired for eating a customer's order of frankfurters. He was also a bellhop at the Hotel Seville. For extra money he walked the dog of a theatrical star. He set pins in a bowling alley, took odd jobs in the garment district, and worked in a shipping brokerage. He also worked briefly for several department stores, including Wanamaker's, where he was fired when caught in a crap game. The object was always to "goof off" as much as possible.

The most famous, or infamous, job Harpo had came after Chico taught him how to make money playing piano in beer gardens. Chico had been performing in beer joints and nickelodeons, including one at which he replaced an unknown named George Gershwin. Harpo subsequently answered an ad and was hired by a Mrs. Schang to play his limited piano repertoire in a whorehouse in Freeport, Long Island. It later turned out that the ubiquitous Chico had previously worked there, too, but had been bounced for some extra-curricular activity. Harpo had to leave for a less glamorous reason: he came down with measles. He left in time to avoid the embarrassment of being connected with the arrest of Mrs. Schang and others on charges involving the use of the house as a headquarters for robbery and the receipt of stolen property.

Groucho had more serious aspirations. For a time he thought about being a doctor, but that was an impractical dream because of the family's poverty. More realistic was his longing to be a writer, a goal which he eventually fulfilled to some extent, when fame as an entertainer brought him the opportunity to write books, articles, and even co-author a play and screenplay. He enjoyed reading, and developed his position as the most intellectual member of the family.

He also learned to sing, practicing at first during musical evenings at home, with Frenchie on the mandolin, Gummo and Minnie on guitars, and Chico on the piano. On Sundays he would sing soprano in a choir at an Episcopal church on Madison Avenue. The picture of Groucho as a boy soprano boggles the mind when one thinks of him croaking the "Captain Spaulding" lyrics in *Animal Crackers*.

Being more serious-minded didn't prevent Groucho from learning to be an operator in the footsteps of his brothers. Groucho has even admitted that he chiseled his own family. His mother would give him five pennies to buy bread. A day-old loaf could be bought for four. Groucho kept the family supplied with day-old bread and himself supplied with extra money. Another way he earned a bit of extra money was getting lunch for a

teacher, who gave him all of one dollar to run the errands for an entire semester.

Groucho never shared Chico's confidence in the pursuit of girls, and this might be important in tracing his penchant for making women the butt of his jokes, on stage and off. Groucho is fond of telling one story from his youthful exploits that surely contains ample material for personality analysis. At the age of twelve, he took a fancy to a girl upstairs. When he saved exactly enough money to take her to Hammerstein's Victoria Theatre for a vaudeville show, he asked her for the date. But Groucho didn't calculate the five cents for the candy she would want.

When they got out of the show, it was dark, cold, and a snowstorm was raging. Groucho had only one nickel left for a streetcar home. He confronted the girl with his predicament, claimed the financial embarrassment was because she had wanted the candy, and said he would toss her to see who got the nickel for a ride home. She lost, so he hopped the streetcar and let her walk. It would take a psychiatrist to pronounce judgment on how much insecurity and hostility was wrapped up in that streetcar ride, but the incident fits snugly into Groucho's comedy persona.

Despite his love of reading, Groucho decided to leave school after his Bar Mitzvah. He didn't

seem to have much trouble convincing his mother that he and a formal education should have a parting of the ways. At thirteen, Groucho quit to take a job as an office boy for the munificent sum of $3.50 per week. Again, his demise in the job was like a scene from a Marx Brothers film. His task was to answer phones, but as the boss spent progressively less time in the office, so did Groucho. One day while he was absent without leave, he made the mistake of picking up a hat that had blown away and returning it to the owner, who, of course, turned out to be the boss. Groucho's mother sent him back to school, until he was rescued by an opportunity in vaudeville.

Gummo and Zeppo, being the youngest, were very much the adjuncts in the family hierarchy. It later turned out that way in show business, too, with neither of them having the affinity for the stage that their brothers had developed under the steamroller tactics of their mother. Because Chico, Harpo, and Groucho became the biggest stars, most of the material that has appeared over the years has concentrated on their stories, from childhood on, and Gummo and Zeppo have been largely lost in the shuffle. But Gummo revealed one little-known fact about himself in an interview with Richard Anobile in *The Marx Bros. Scrapbook*. He recalls his problem of stammering

as a child, a handicap which reappeared even when he thought he had defeated it. Performing held built-in terror.

The early milieu of the Marx Brothers was peopled with a host of film-like characters adding to the general mayhem. Not the least was Uncle Carl, who worked for a gang of arsonists. His job was to set fire to resort hotels which had seen better days, so that the owners could thereby collect insurance. Carl spent five years in prison. Inevitably there was a meddling rent collector, a Mr. Hummel, whose most difficult task was even finding a Marx. Since Minnie was such a warm-hearted person, visitors would drop in when the family wasn't in hiding, and the Marxes were surrounded by the kind of tumult that undoubtedly added to their flair for making the most out of chaos.

Apart from Minnie, the most important person in the launching of their professional life was their uncle, Al Shean. A cherubic little man with a wide smile and twinkling eyes, he was Minnie's first success at plotting show business careers. Al had worked as a pants presser, but his hobby was singing. Minnie acted as his agent and got him into vaudeville, and he eventually rose to the top as part of the popular team of Gallagher and Shean. They became a phenomenal success, and their lines "Positively, Mr. Gallagher . . . Absolutely, Mr. Shean" became something of a national byword. A visit from Uncle Al was an event.

He dressed nattily in the fashions of the day, and every time he called, which was about once a month, he would give each of the boys a dime when he left. Later, he raised it to twenty cents, then a quarter. Al was indeed a success, and he carried with him the aura of a glamorous show business career. He made a deep impression on the young Marxes, and the fact that their mother had been responsible for seeing that Al made much of his talent set the stage for the fulfillment of the rest of her dream.

REHEARSAL FOR THE MOVIES

The grubby, grueling trail of the vaudeville circuit in the early part of this century is well known. Many show business figures traveled this road, and it was the path the Marx Brothers took before their glory years. It took about a decade for the brothers to evolve into a top-flight success. The feat was accomplished by trial and error and combinations of circumstance, with bits and pieces coming together to form the peculiar brand of comedy their fans now recognize. Their early years of performing are instructive and revealing, virtually a rehearsal for the films, for that is where the crucial shaping took place.

They were tough years, fully in the tradition of the legends about itinerant entertainers. There were managers who didn't pay. Hustlers who absconded with wages. Hostile audiences who threw things. Flea-bag hotels. Inedible food. And fleeing from irate fathers and angry husbands whose daughters and wives had been seduced. Broke more often than not, the Marxes had to work in an atmosphere of cutthroat competition between the sharp, ruthless managers of the various touring circuits. Add to all of this the propensity for the Marx Brothers themselves to stir things up and one has some idea of the hectic period these years were for the stars-to-be.

Groucho's first brush with touring came when he applied for a job as a boy singer for $4 a week plus room and board to perform in Michigan and Colorado as part of a trio. He thought he was flying high. Apart from the fact that the act was dreadful, the entrepreneur disappeared with Groucho's money in Cripple Creek, Colorado. Groucho had to sell his costume to pay the rent, and he took the unlikely job of driving a horse and wagon. After making his way back to New York, Groucho was helped into another tour by his mother. This time he was boy singer for an English actress. A companion act on the tour featured a lion tamer. The actress ran away with the tamer, and they were also accompanied by Groucho's money.

Chico's entrance into vaudeville was as accompanist for a cousin, Lou Shean. While Lou sang, Chico would wear a blindfold and play the piano. After Lou dropped out, Chico did a single, playing audience requests blindfolded and with a bedsheet over the keyboard.

Harpo got his stage baptism when Gummo, Groucho, and a friend named Lou Levy were singing in a trio in a Coney Island beer garden called Henderson's. Minnie decided to convert the trio into a quartet after she bought four white

HORSE FEATHERS (1932). Groucho and his inevitable cigar, with Robert Greig

duck suits for the price of three. At fourteen Harpo went before an audience, and the thought of having to sing must have been too much for him. He wet his pants on stage.

Minnie, by now an expert at putting together acts to meet the needs of the moment, had Gummo, Groucho, and a girl singer working as The Three Nightingales. A boy singer replaced the girl and Harpo was added, making it The Four Nightingales. This boon to the entertainment world eventually gave way to the Six Mascots, with Minnie and her sister Hannah joining the act for a while. (Having more family members helped at times when the pay would be figured according to the number of performers.) Chico didn't join the Marx contingent until it was well into touring. For a while he worked as a song-plugger in Pittsburgh, and he traveled with his own act before joining the family. Gummo stuck with it until he went into the army in World War I, a timely excuse to get out of a profession he disliked. Zeppo moved up to take his place.

In the beginning the emphasis was primarily on singing, with back-up dancing by pretty girls hired to brighten the show. There was only a smattering of comedy, which grew until it became the mainstay of the act. Gradually, the familiar Groucho-Chico-Harpo comedy style emerged, receiving its greatest impetus during a performance in Champaign, Illinois, when a singer who wanted more money left the act. Groucho's son Arthur, in his book *Son of Groucho*, traces his father's use of ad-libs to an incident in Texas. The episode also accelerated the development of the brothers toward roughhouse comedy.

The act was booked into a honky-tonk theater in Nacogdoches, Texas, and one matinée the audience started leaving to watch more promising entertainment in the form of a runaway mule. They returned half an hour later to hear the singing Marxes. The brothers decided to get even by doing a takeoff on their songs, and they started horsing around and insulting the Texans. Groucho threw in lines like "Nacogdoches is full of roaches," and "The jackass is the finest flower of Tex-ass." The brothers aroused more laughter than ire, and the crowd loved their antics. Word about them spread, and by the time they played Denison, Texas, the manager agreed to pay them $74 instead of $50 for the act if they would use more comedy. Since a teacher's convention was in town, Groucho suggested a school routine, which was the beginning of the act that carried the Marxes all the way to the coveted Palace, the legendary vaudeville mecca in New York City. Later one would find a more sophisticated extension,

ANIMAL CRACKERS (1930). Harpo and Chico clearly baffle Margaret Dumont and Margaret Irving. Note Harpo's horn.

college style, in *Horse Feathers*.

School acts were popular then. Gus Edwards did the most famous one, "School Days," and others copied the material. The Marx Brothers (Groucho, Harpo, and Gummo at the time) called theirs "Fun in Hi Skule." Groucho donned a frock coat for the first time, and he wore a black, fake mustache. (Later he painted on a mustache when he couldn't find the fake one, and argued with a manager who insisted he was paying for a "real" mustache. But the painted one proved as funny and Groucho found that easier to handle.)

Harpo played a dumbbell type, known in the vaudeville vernacular of the day as a Patsy Brannigan character. He wore a wig made out of old rope. Gummo was more of a straight man since he was the best-looking of the trio. Ultimately their act was improved by Uncle Al Shean, who wrote a second sketch called "Mr. Green's Reception," built around a class reunion, with Groucho as old Mr. Green, whom his former pupils come back to see.

Still later, Shean wrote an act called "Home Again," which evolved from "Mr. Green's Reception." It was "Home Again" that brought the Marx Brothers their

LOVE HAPPY (1949). Chico with Ilona Massey, still "chick chasing"

greatest fame up to that time and gave them the kind of high-class act that enabled them to play the Palace and the most sought after theaters of the day. It must be remembered that in the era of vaudeville, performers played the same act and sketches for years, since they traveled to so many different theaters and material did not become instantly stale as it does now when seen on television by millions in one performance.

Many of the familiar characteristics of the Marx Brothers films can be traced to the vaudeville grind. Groucho, in addition to practicing the art of ad-libbing, picked up the idea of wielding a cigar from other comedians who taught him that a cigar made a handy stage prop. You could use it to wait for laughs, or to get laughs, or have it handy in the event you forgot a line. Dialect comedy being "in" at the time, Groucho experimented with German, while Chico specialized in Italian.

Harpo didn't start as a silent clown. He had dialogue, but wasn't particularly good with it, and he was given increasingly less to say. One critic in Illinois complained that Harpo should stick to his pantomime. Uncle Al felt the same way and the silent Harpo emerged. This made it necessary for him to find new ways to get laughs without talking. Once he stole a bulb-type horn from a taxi, and we know the

outcome of that. In San Francisco, when it was raining, Harpo bought a second-hand raincoat for three dollars. It fell apart, but he kept it for the act, lining the coat with pockets large enough to hide props that could be produced on stage to the delight of audiences. The coat went well with a battered hat and his red wig.

Harpo began using a harp in the act while it was known as the Six Mascots. Minnie provided him with a second-hand instrument which Al Shean bought. Harpo practiced diligently for a year before he performed a full solo. Gummo has recalled that Harpo learned how to tune the instrument himself, but that it was tuned off key. He learned to play accordingly, and kept doing it that way even in films. Harpo was in a train accident with his first harp. The case was smashed, but the harp was undamaged. Harpo slyly took care of that. He tossed the harp onto the tracks so that it was also battered, and then, with the help of a lawyer, received a substantial enough insurance settlement to buy a new and better one.

The nicknames by which the brothers are known are credited to a vaudeville monologist named Art Fisher. There have been various stories about how the Marxes got their names, but this one seems the most authentic. It was stylish to have names ending in "o" because of a popular comic strip of the period called "Knocko and Monk." While in Rockford, Illinois, the brothers were playing poker with Fisher, who began referring to them as Harpo because of his harp, Chico, because of his "chick-chasing," Groucho because of his disposition, and Gummo because he wore gum-soled shoes and could walk up quietly behind people like a "gumshoe," or detective.

The brothers began using the names on the stage. A typesetter mistakenly dropped the "k" from Chico, so his name was kept that way. When brother Herbert came into the act, he was called Zippo after a chimp trainer named "Mr. Zippo." But Herbert didn't like the association, according to Harpo, and switched to Zeppo.

During these days of cross-country traveling, the Marx brothers rubbed shoulders with others who were to achieve fame or were already well known. In a Waukegan, Illinois theater, a violin player in the pit orchestra was Benny Kubelsky, who later became known as Jack Benny. They subsequently appeared on the same bills with Benny. In Winnipeg and Vancouver they encountered Charlie Chaplin doing his act, "A Night At the Club." Groucho recalls being on the bill with W. C. Fields, who allegedly quit because he hated to follow the madcap routine of the Marxes with his juggling act. Later in their career they were on a bill with Sarah Bernhardt. At one point the Marxes toured with popular boxer Benny Leonard.

Their collective experiences as itinerant comics are worth an entire book. They may have played as many as three hundred cities and towns and in most of them, Chico was the one who got into trouble. Once he stole a Salvation Army bass drum, which he promptly pawned to come up with money he owed. In Scranton, Pennsylvania, a group of coal miners were after the brothers because one of them had found his daughter and Chico making love. One show was done without Chico because he fled to Canada to save his life—he had given a bad check to a gangster. Chico had a knack for such involvements. He once played cards in Chicago with a guy who became an Al Capone bodyguard. Groucho was no slouch himself. Once, in Muncie, Indiana, he hid in a closet and then jumped out of a window with a fifteen-foot drop, to avoid a husband who had interrupted his tryst.

Before reaching the Palace, the Marxes achieved popularity on the touring circuits. By the time "Home Again" played New York area theaters of the Keith Circuit, the Marx brothers were getting a total of $1500 weekly for their act.

But their first booking at the

33

Palace almost never took place. In 1915 vaudeville tycoon E. F. Albee booked them for both the Palace and a prior week at the Royal. But the Albee office wasn't satisfied, and the Palace stint was called off. Albee, however, didn't reckon with Minnie. She wouldn't take no for an answer and finally the booking was reinstated. To express his reluctance, Albee had the brothers placed in the most undesirable spot of opening the show. But they were so uproarious that nobody else wanted to follow them, and they worked their way up to the closing spot.

Variety called "Home Again" a vaudeville act that "the big time could depend upon for a feature" in a review of their debut at the Royal. The review of February 12, 1915 said: "The fun-making is taken care of by three of the Marx brothers. Julius takes the elderly role (Henry Schneider) and is an excellent German comedian. Leonard Marx is the Italian, who plays the piano in trick and other ways, also has comedy scenes with his brother, Arthur Marx. The latter is in what the program says is a nondescript role. This Arthur Marx is marked as a comedian for a Broadway show, just as certain as you are reading this. He is a comedian who doesn't talk. Arthur plays the harp and piano, getting laughs from his handling of both. . . . Arthur made the house laugh any time he wanted

them to."

The opening at the Palace was described by *Billboard* as follows: "Their tabloid ran forty minutes, and during that time the audience was either rocking with laughter or electrified with applause." The act was a large one, with twelve people in addition to the four brothers.

During the vaudeville period that led to their ultimate triumph at the Palace, the Marx brothers were developing the type of comedy that later characterized their films, and they were moving toward the hit status on Broadway that made their films possible. But even after reaching the top in vaudeville, it wasn't all smooth sailing. After enjoying a substantial period of public and financial success, the brothers had a falling out with Albee that led to their being blacklisted, and, ironically, to their triumph in the Broadway theater.

Conflicting versions of what happened involve fights over money and their going to work in London without Albee's permission. In any event, Albee refused to have them working on his circuit, and his power was such that the performers had to work with a smaller act, taking what bookings they could snare. For a while they worked for the rival Shubert unit, which was more demanding, and which folded shortly after the brothers joined it. Necessity opened the key door.

As in his films, Chico was a

SAM H. HARRIS

PRESENTS

The

MARX·BROTHERS

IN

THE COCOANUTS

A MUSICAL COMEDY

MUSIC AND LYRICS BY
IRVING
BERLIN

BOOK BY
GEO. S. KAUFMAN

DANCE NUMBERS BY SAMMY LEE

BOOK DIRECTED BY
OSCAR EAGLE

sharp hustler with the ability to manipulate people. Harpo relates that Chico, while playing cards, met a producer, who came up with a backer, one Herman Broody, of Hackensack, New Jersey. To the brothers' good fortune, Broody was involved with a girl eager to be in a show. The brothers managed to get $25,000 from him, which enabled them to put together a musical called *I'll Say She Is*. Although it was a broad mixture of familiar material, the show did very well, and was parlayed into a run of about a year and a half on tour. In Philadelphia alone, it played more than four months. Today producers of musicals like to cash in on extensive tours before coming to New York to face the critics. The same principle operated with *I'll Say She Is*, but after being on the road for so long, it became logical to give Broadway a try. The date which now looms so large was May 19, 1924.

The opening of *I'll Say She Is* at the Casino Theatre was considered appropriate for second-string reviewers. As luck would have it for the Marx brothers, a show that was to have been given reviewing priority was postponed and the caustic Alexander Woollcott, considered the most powerful Broadway critic of his day, was free to turn his skepticism on the Marx Brothers. He took an influential friend, newspaper columnist Franklin P.

Adams, with him. Woollcott was bowled over, particularly by Harpo. He wrote in the *New York Sun*:

"As one of the many who laughed immoderately throughout the greater part of the first New York performance given by a new musical show, entitled, if memory serves, *I'll Say She Is*, it behooves your correspondent to report at once that that harlequinade has some of the most comical moments vouchsafed to the first-nighters in a month of Mondays. It is a bright colored and vehement setting for the goings on of those talented cutups, the Four Marx Brothers. In particular, it is a splendacious and reasonably tuneful excuse for going to see that silent brother, that shy, unexpected, magnificent comic among the Marxes, who is recorded somewhere on a birth certificate as Adolph, but who is known to the adoring two-a-day as Harpo Marx.

"Surely there should be dancing in the streets when a great clown comes to town, and this man is a great clown. He is officially billed as a member of the Marx family, but truly he belongs to that greater family which includes Joe Jackson and Bert Melrose and the Fratillini brothers. Harpo Marx, so styled, oddly enough, because he plays the harp, says never a word from first to last, but when by merely leaning against one's brother one can seem richly and irresistibly amusing, why should one speak?"

Now Minnie's dream had really come true. She had to be carried on a stretcher into the Casino Theatre for the opening, since she had a fractured leg. But she saw the culmination of those years of struggling. In addition to Woollcott, other leading critics of the day were also impressed. The word of Percy Hammond, Heywood Broun, George S. Kaufman, and George Jean Nathan carried weight.

Incredibly, Harpo, the kid who was tossed out of a school window and had no formal education, became the darling of the literary set in New York. He became a regular at the "Round Table," the name for the coterie of intellectuals who gathered at the Algonquin Hotel to trade witticisms and put the world in its place. Woollcott was a leading light, and among those who joined in the verbal jousting at various times were such luminaries as Dorothy Parker, Harold Ross, George S. Kaufman and his wife Beatrice, Ring Lardner, Tallulah Bankhead, Robert Benchley, Franklin P. Adams, Robert Sherwood, Herman Mankiewicz, Heywood Broun, Deems Taylor, Donald Ogden Stewart, and Alice Duer Miller.

Woollcott, with whom Harpo developed a close friendship that lasted until the critic's death, got Harpo into a club of literary poker players. Known as the Thanatopsis Club, it included Benchley, Swope, Adams, Broun, Kaufman, Ross, and Marc Connelly. Harpo was a prized companion. He also introduced Chico to the club, but it was Harpo who became the regular. In general, the brothers became celebrities about town and were the recipients of a barrage of publicity. Their colorful antics offstage gave them an additional reputation to live up to.

The Marx brothers were now major stage stars, and the problem was how to produce another hit with them. *The Cocoanuts*, which opened December 8, 1925, filled the bill. Now more famous names were involved. Irving Berlin wrote the music, and George S. Kaufman wrote the book, which lightly satirized the land boom in Florida. The producer was Sam Harris, who reputedly told Berlin that "Always," one of his songs meant for the show, wasn't any good. It was not used, and neither was some of the other Berlin music that kept being eliminated in the cutting of the show. *The Cocoanuts* ran for a year on Broadway, and then was successful in a two-year national tour.

Their third straight hit was *Animal Crackers*, produced in the fall of 1928, with a book by Kaufman and Morrie Ryskind. This time music and lyrics were by Bert Kalmar and Harry Ruby. The experience on Broadway did nothing to curb the appetite of the Marx brothers for spontaneity. Arthur Marx recalls that as a boy he would be taken backstage, where he would watch his father and uncles in *Animal Crackers*, and that one day Groucho carried him on stage in a sedan chair during a performance. Groucho also helped columnist Walter Winchell circumvent his being barred from seeing the show because of a feud Winchell was having with the Shuberts. Groucho dressed Winchell in one of Harpo's get-ups, including a red wig, and put him in the wings to watch in the guise of an understudy. One famous line by George S. Kaufman was reportedly uttered while watching a performance of *Animal Crackers*. He is supposed to have said to Woollcott, "Be quiet a minute, Alex, I think I just heard one of the original lines."

The crash of 1929 occurred while *Animal Crackers* was running on Broadway. Groucho, who had amassed a considerable amount of money and invested it in stocks, was wiped out. He was thoroughly downcast by the financial catastrophe, but had to continue playing the clown. Chico was less bereft—he had been losing his money all along through gambling.

Fortunately for the Marx Brothers—and for movie buffs—the film industry was already beginning to blossom with the newest innovation, talkies. A whole new world was opening up, and one didn't have to look beyond what the Marxes had already done on Broadway for the vehicles to their film fame.

On stage in THE COCOANUTS (1925)

Today fans of the Marx brothers read all manner of significance into their film comedy. But the brothers could scarcely have envisioned their pictures being studied and analyzed by film students and gaining increasing stature as comedy classics in a medium which has since come to be considered as the great art form of the twentieth century.

At the outset of the Marx careers, films were primarily a burgeoning and lucrative form of show business. With talkies as the latest craze, producers began looking around for talent to exploit in order to make the most of the money-making gimmick at hand. Broadway was an obvious source for both talent and script material. With comedy a prized commodity, it was logical that the funniest performers in the New York theater would be prime candidates for filmmaking.

Paramount Pictures signed the Marx Brothers to a three-film contract at $75,000 per picture, and the first one to be made was *The Cocoanuts*, based on their stage success. Since *Animal Crackers* was still a hit, going to California was out of the question, and it was decided that the film would be made in the spring of 1929 in the Paramount Studios at Astoria, Long Island. It would be possible for the Marx Brothers to do the picture during the day and appear on stage at night. There were no lofty

PARAMOUNT YEARS

ideas of turning out anything exceptional from a cinematic viewpoint. The immediate task was to get the stage comedy on film quickly, and since it had been so successful, to stick closely to the original and retain as many laughs as possible. They plunged into the making of *The Cocoanuts* with a thorough knowledge of what audiences had found funny.

Actually, this was not the first Marx Brothers experience before a camera. They had already made a silent movie called *Humorisk*, but they are said to have subsequently destroyed it. Cheaply produced, it was shown at a matinée in the Bronx, and then disappeared. Groucho was apparently the bad guy in the film, Harpo a hero in love, and Mildred Davis was the girl playing opposite Harpo.

In 1925 Harpo appeared in a film with Richard Dix. It was called *Too Many Kisses* and Harpo was cast as a village idiot, but most of his mugging wound up on the cutting room floor. He was only seen briefly, and when the picture was reviewed in *The New York Times*, Harpo made the credits, but wasn't mentioned in the review, which described the film as "a constantly amusing light entertainment."

The Cocoanuts, evaluated in retrospect, assumes a special

39

The Four Marx Brothers at Paramount

character, since it stands as the first recorded opportunity to observe what the antics of the brothers were like at that moment of their stage popularity. It also tells us much about the limitations of filmmaking at the time. But this very stiffness of style in the film preserves an approximate portrait of what their Broadway production must have been like, a quality which could have been lost had there been any cinematic "opening up" of their show. Of course, the antics changed along the way to the extent that the Marxes ad-libbed, but the film can be accepted as a reasonable replica of the stage production.

The awkwardness is particularly apparent when plot and romance take over. Contemporary audiences accustomed to more sophistication now break into laughter at the cloying sincerity of romantically smitten leading man Oscar Shaw as Bob Adams, mooning over Mary Eaton as heroine Polly Potter. The musical numbers become more campy with the passing years, but they typified the obligatory sequences in the emerging film musicals.

What worked best was the comedy, and that is what producer Walter Wanger and directors Robert Florey and Joseph Santley relied upon. The paucity of creativity can be seen in the remark by Florey, who recalled some forty-five years later: "Aside from directing traffic, which turned out to be my main function, I photographed

THE COCOANUTS (1929). With Zeppo, Kay Francis, Groucho, Cyril Ring, and Margaret Dumont

THE COCOANUTS (1929). A very brief altercation

it to the best of my ability." Florey worked under the handicap of never having seen the Marx Brothers in the stage version of *The Cocoanuts*. But he did get a look at *Animal Crackers*. A further handicap was that Florey was never enthusiastic about the assignment; it was not the type of film he really wanted to direct. In addition, the conditions were trying. Keeping the Marx Brothers in line so that their antics didn't disrupt the schedule was problem enough. But there was the enormous technical challenge involved in the new sound medium. Since *The Cocoanuts* was one of the earliest sound films, there were many new problems that had to be solved on the basis of what amounted to trial and error.

Morrie Ryskind, who wrote the screen adaptation, put it this way: "If a fly buzzed on the set, it sounded like an airplane." There was a minimum of rehearsing for the film, which was shot within a month. For the Marx Brothers themselves, the task was made easier by their having done the show so many times on stage. The joy of any Marx film lies in its anarchy, not in its plot construction. It is a tribute to those who made the film that they managed to preserve this sense of anarchy.

The Florida land boom under way at the time was the peg on which the plot was hung, centering on young architect Bob Adams' plan to develop the Cocoanut Grove area. Added to the idea of real estate development is Bob's romance with Polly Potter and a scheme by which villain Harvey Yates would steal a necklace from Polly's wealthy mother. This was considered a sufficient background against which the Marxes could carry on. Groucho, wearing his greasepaint mustache, and frock coat, and wielding his trusty cigar, is operating a questionable Florida hotel. Chico and Harpo are satirical versions of the kind of charlatans who might gravitate toward Groucho.

Mrs. Potter is played by the inimitable Margaret Dumont, probably the best foil comedy ever had. She was in the stage version of *The Cocoanuts*, and at the time the film was made, was also appearing in *Animal Crackers*. The picture also affords an interesting look at Kay Francis in her second film, playing a sexy, conniving woman in cahoots with the villain. As for Zeppo, never was his adjunct status more apparent. His part is barely there at all, as if he had to be somehow tenuously connected with the enterprise to keep peace in the family.

Sensitive to Zeppo's perpetual plight in the Marx galaxy, critic Percy Hammond wrote in the *Herald-Tribune*, after seeing *Animal Crackers* on stage, suggesting that Zeppo might be more appreciated if he could perform on his own. Hammond wrote: "One of the handicaps to thorough enjoyment

of the Marx brothers in their merry escapades is the plight of poor Zeppo Marx. While Groucho, Harpo and Chico are hogging the show, as the phrase has it, their brother hides in an insignificant role, peeping out now and then to listen to plaudits in which he has no share . . . . When, if ever, he is noticed by the press, it is with disdain. Reviewers have said of him that he makes the Marx quartet a trio, and that he is but an appendage to a fraternity already overloaded." The film version of *The Cocoanuts* does nothing to change that image.

Some of the gags in the film are indicative of the freedom that prevailed at the time in comparison with the crackdown to come later when Hollywood became more sensitive to pressure groups. Groucho, renting a hotel room to Chico: "Would you take a suite on the third floor?" Chico: "No, we'd like a Polack in the basement." At another point, Groucho and Chico look over the blueprints for the proposed development. Groucho: "Those are all the levees." Chico: "That's-a the Jewish neighborhood." Groucho: "Well, we'll Passover that."

The blueprint routine presented problems. The blueprints had to be soaked to keep them from crackling and ruining the sound. Once under way, the results were worth the effort. Groucho: "Here's Cocoanut Manor and here's Co-

THE COCOANUTS (1929). Harpo with Mary Eaton

ANIMAL CRACKERS (1930). Enter Captain Spaulding

coanut Heights—it's a swamp, and here, where the road forks, is Cocoanut Junction." Chico: "Where's Cocoanut custard?" Groucho: "Over by the forks." This routine includes the classic "why-a-duck" line. When Groucho points to the location of the viaduct, Chico further confuses matters: "Why-a-duck, why-a no chicken?"

Another Marxism found in *The Cocoanuts*: Groucho to Dumont: "Did anyone ever tell you you look like the Prince of Wales? I don't mean the present Prince of Wales. One of the old Wales. And believe me when I say whales, I mean whales. I know a whale when I see one."

This formula of patter was to be repeated, expanded, milked, and exploited to the hilt in future films. The problem in commiting it to film, along with other verbal or sight gags, was that anybody on the set, including the director, might be prone to break up during the shooting. Harpo later speculated in his autobiography that a film about the making of *The Cocoanuts* might have been funnier than the film. He may have a point. Director Florey would laugh so hard that the sound track would be ruined. The producer solved this problem by having Florey placed inside a glass booth from which he could give signals.

There was also another major

46

problem. Chico, with gambling on his mind and the need to reach his bookie, would suddenly disappear and not come back in time for the next scene, if at all. This problem was solved by locking Chico in one of the jail cells being used for the picture. A phone was put in the cell so Chico would be able to lose his money from there. "When shooting resumed," said Harpo, "the directors were put back into their glass cage and the stars were let out of their jail cells."

Despite such chaotic conditions, the picture was finished and it opened to acclaim at the Rialto Theater in May, 1929. But the review in *The New York Times* seemed somewhat more concerned with the use of sound in filmmaking than with the content of the picture itself. Critic Mordaunt Hall, finding "considerable merriment," called the film "an audible pictorial transcription of the musical comedy, *The Cocoanuts.*"

The New Yorker, less awed by sound and more involved in the comedy, saw the film as "one of the funniest pictures in many seasons" and added of the Marxes, "their peculiar talents seem, surprisingly enough, even more manifest on the screen than on stage. In their antics there is that stuff which makes the convulsing, uproarious laughter associated in our memory with the early Chaplin pictures . . ."

The Cocoanuts turned out to be the only Marx Brothers film that Minnie Marx saw. She died at sixty-five on September 13, 1929, when her sons were preparing to take *Animal Crackers* on tour. She suffered a stroke following a family party and died that night. Harpo touchingly recalled the trauma of the moment when she briefly recognized him, managed to smile, her lips trembling and her eyes fearful. "Her fingertips fluttered against the bedcover," Harpo remembered: "She was trying to say something. I knew what she was trying to say. I reached over and straightened her wig, the new blond wig she had bought especially for tonight. The smile came back for a second. Then it faded, and all the life in Minnie faded with it. I took her into my arms. I don't remember what I said, or thought. I only remember I was crying."*

But Minnie had lived to see the start of the film career that would preserve for future generations the fruits of her long labors to make her sons stars. *The Cocoanuts*, popular with the public, added to the enchantment with talkies, and made the Marxes full-fledged film stars, ready to cash in on their popularity by committing *Animal Crackers* to the screen, another logical step in view of its status as a stage hit.

The Marx Brothers were well-

Harpo Speaks!, p. 274

prepared for the filming of *Animal Crackers*. As with *The Cocoanuts*, they had played it *ad infinitum* before audiences, both on Broadway and on tour. They invaded the Astoria studios of Paramount again, and the procedure was similar. No fancy cinematic transformations. The task was essentially to reproduce on screen what had clicked on stage.

Morrie Ryskind provided another screenplay, but this time Hollywood director Victor Heerman, who had worked for Mack Sennett, was put in charge, and the music and lyrics were supplied by Bert Kalmar and Harry Ruby. As had been the case with the filming of *The Cocoanuts*, there were cast changes from the original version. But foil Margaret Dumont was there, as regally unflappable as ever. Retrospectively, the most illustrious addition to the screen roster turned out to be Lillian Roth as ingenue Arabella Rittenhouse.

Animal Crackers has the distinction of containing Groucho's best-known song "Hooray for Captain Spaulding." Groucho makes one of his most majestic film entrances as Captain Jeffrey T. Spaulding, noted African explorer. Appropri-

ANIMAL CRACKERS (1930). *Groucho, Margaret Dumont, and a bemused party guest*

ANIMAL CRACKERS (1930). Groucho is about to trade blows with Louis Sorin, to Margaret Dumont's dismay.

ANIMAL CRACKERS (1930). Chico and Harpo square off for some fisticuffs.

ately he is borne into the mansion of Mrs. Rittenhouse (Margaret Dumont) by African "natives." Greeted with the proper acclaim, he takes over the scene and gets laughs with his explorer's get-up, topped by a white hat with chinstrap. An examination of a photo from the stage version indicates more outlandish casting of the bearers than in the film. Apparently there was an effort to make the film "classier" looking.

But Groucho was Groucho, tossing off such lines from the Captain Spaulding song as "Hello, I must be going—I cannot stay I came to say I must be going—I'm glad I came but just the same I must be going." When the chorus sings, "The captain is a moral man. If he hears anything obscene, he'll naturally repel it," Groucho chimes in: "I hate a dirty joke I do, unless it's told by someone who knows how to tell it."

In *Animal Crackers* the verbal assault by Groucho on Dumont is further honed to hostile perfection. Groucho: "You've got beauty,

ANIMAL CRACKERS (1930). Harpo and horn

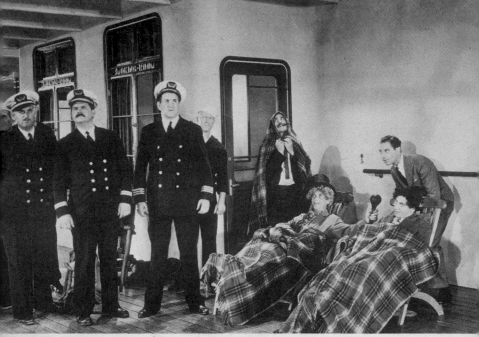

MONKEY BUSINESS (1931). The ship's officers looking for some obvious stowaways

charm, money. You have got money, haven't you? If you haven't, we can quit right now. Ever since I met you I've swept you off my feet. Something has been throbbing within me like an incessant tom-tom in the primitive jungle. There's something I must ask you. Would you wash out a pair of socks for me?"

The good captain's first speech to his assembled admirers contains some of Groucho's most famous and outrageous lines: "One morning I shot an elephant in my pajamas. How he got into my pajamas I'll never know. Then we tried to remove the tusks, but they were imbedded so firmly that we couldn't budge them. Of course, in Alabama the Tuskaloosa. But that's entirely irrelephant."

Puns, double entendres, non sequiturs, and mangling of the language are mixed with sight gags for superbly comic results. But the film also suffers from poor pacing and a heaviness in spots. The plot is as silly as in any of the Marx films. Mrs. Rittenhouse is to unveil a famous painting, *The Hunt*, and Arabella plots to substitute a copy made by her artist boyfriend in the hope that he will be given acclaim when his true talent is revealed. Chico is a musician, Harpo a professor, so to speak, and Zeppo is the captain's secretary. The party that Mrs.

Rittenhouse gives becomes a lunatic affair as the brothers turn nonsense into gold.

When the film was reissued in 1974, audiences didn't seem to mind the awkward aspects. A new generation took to the comic high spots with new devotion, and those with fond memories had them stirred once more, and were quite willing to overlook the negative elements. Besides, the chance to hear the Captain Spaulding song again was especially welcome.

Animal Crackers opened in New York in August, 1930, at the Rialto, the same theater in which *The Cocoanuts* had premiered. Contending that the stage-to-screen transfer was more successful than with *The Cocoanuts*, *The New Yorker* commented: "Harpo and Groucho carry the piece (Carry it? They bounce it all over the place) and with the crackling Kaufman lines they leave you after a good hour and a half like something run through a wringer. It's a very exhausting humor, but the hangover is slight, and the fun is worth it."

Mordaunt Hall reviewed the film in *The New York Times* with a peculiar casualness. Most of the review was concerned with plot

MONKEY BUSINESS (1931). Chico watches as Harpo throws a "Gookie"

description, about the least important element in a Marx film. The review began:

"The Marx Brothers are to be seen at the Rialto in a further example of amusing nonsense, this time the audible film of *Animal Crackers*. This mad affair suits the principals and its absurdities brought forth gales of laughter yesterday afternoon. It is, however, the sort of thing that will only appeal to those who revel in the work of these four brothers."

This sort of condescension was something the Marx Brothers encountered along with the adulation. Their deviltry, loaded with sight-gags, was looked down upon by some who thought silliness beneath them. Many critics felt compelled to warn readers that they might not belong to the group addicted to the brothers. But through the years, the cult that developed wore down the resistance of many holdouts.

Freed of their stage commitments, in 1931 the Marxes were available to head for the heart of movieland itself. Paramount wanted them in Hollywood to continue their picture-making. The move marked a turning point. *The Cocoanuts* and *Animal Crackers* were reruns of their theatrical success. Now they would join the Hollywood mill and become film stars subject to the pressures and uncertainties that plagued others in the business.

The foremost problem faced in creating other pictures was getting fresh material suitable to the Marxes and finding writers who could ape their style. The comedians, while new to Hollywood, had an inkling of the danger of drying up the well of material, and they decided against doing more than one picture a year. Jesse Lasky of Paramount hired a battery of writers to begin working on a new Marx script. Groucho recruited Will B. Johnstone, who had written *I'll Say She Is*. He was impressed by S. J. Perelman, then known primarily as a cartoonist, and he also found talent in a sketch by Nat Perrin, who was a law student with writing aspirations. Perrin was originally hired as Chico's gagwriter. Arthur Sheekman, a Chicago newspaper columnist, was another addition, assigned to writing Groucho's gags.

A comic strip of the time was called "Little Benny," and since it was about a boy unable to speak, what could be more logical than asking its author, J. Carver Pusey, to write sight gags and scenes for Harpo? Herman J. Mankiewicz, who was later to script the classic *Citizen Kane*, was assigned by the studio as producer for the Marx Brothers.

The first result of their long labors fizzled. Perelman read the script at one of those conferences for which Hollywood was famous, and Groucho's pithy comment was,

MONKEY BUSINESS (1931). Chico, Harpo, and victim

"It stinks!" There was more work, various collaborative sessions, and out of this confusion and potpourri of wits, the script for *Monkey Business* ultimately emerged as the first original screenplay for a Marx film. Screenwriting credits went to Perelman and Johnstone, with additional dialogue by Sheekman.

Perelman recalled the tumultuous experience of working on a Marx Brothers picture in *Show* Magazine in 1961: Mankiewicz had warned him that the Marxes were "mercurial, devious and ungrateful. I hate to depress you, but you'll rue the day you ever took the assignment. This is an ordeal by fire. Make sure you wear asbestos pants." When the script was ready Johnstone and Mankiewicz had to

read it to an entourage of twenty-seven people. Perelman added: "It took five months of drudgery and Homeric quarrels, ambuscades and intrigues that would have shamed the Borgias, but it finally reached the camera and the result was *Monkey Business*, a muscular hit."

Groucho has made a point of downgrading the contribution Perelman made, but Perrin disputes him on this. Such hassles tend to obscure past collaborations. But certainly some of the Perelman-type wit abounds in *Monkey Business*. The director assigned to the film was Norman McLeod, who could direct Marx Brothers screen traffic with sufficient competence but didn't prove to be a cinematic innovator. However, there was much more movement now that the film was liberated from the concept of transferring stage plays to the screen.

Missing was Margaret Dumont. Groucho had wanted to give the project a fresh look, and so blonde temptress Thelma Todd became the foil as Lucille, wife of a bootlegger. In this way the comedy was given a different orientation, with more stress on spoofing sex appeal than on mocking high society. The film is nearly one long chase, first as the brothers are discovered stowing away on a ship coming to America, and then when they become involved in the machinations of underworld characters. Along the way is a generous helping of the horseplay, verbal and physical, which the Marxes do so well.

Puns are everywhere. As the brothers are bobbing up and down in the barrels in which they are hiding aboard ship, Chico says: "I was goin' to bring my grandfather, but there's no room for his beard." Groucho: "Why don't you send for the old swine and let his beard come later?" Chico: "I sent for his beard." Groucho: "You did?" Chico: "Yeah, it's coming by hair-mail."

Or Lucille to Groucho: "You're awfully shy for a lawyer." Groucho: "You bet I'm shy. I'm a shyster lawyer." And when a gangster warns Chico, "Keep out of this loft!," Chico retorts: "Well, it's better to have loft and lost than never to have loft at all."

As for action sequences, *Monkey Business* contains many gems. There is a scene in which the brothers take over a barber shop and give a hapless customer the works. In one of their most delightful conning scenes, the brothers are trying to get off the ship with the passport of Maurice Chevalier. Each time a skeptical immigration officer challenges them. Zeppo does a Chevalier imitation, singing the opening lines of "You Brought A New Kind of Love To Me." He is pushed to the back of the line. Chico tries his luck, breaking into the same song. He gets pushed back. Now it is Groucho's turn. A similar rejection. Harpo tries, first offering a piece of pasteboard, then a washboard, before finally showing a passport with Chevalier's picture. Then we hear Chevalier's voice to Harpo's miming and we see that Harpo has a phonograph strapped to his back. It begins to run down, and his ploy is exposed. Bedlam follows, as Harpo seizes an immigration stamp and begins stamping everything in sight, including the officer's bald head.

The brothers make their customary shambles of a party scene, with Harpo hiding in a woman's bustle. When the woman moves away, the bustle remains behind, whereupon Harpo proceeds to attach himself to the dress of a

MONKEY BUSINESS (1931). With Thelma Todd, Groucho, Zeppo, and Harry Woods

woman who is dancing. The finale is a scramble in a barn, as the Marxes break up a kidnapping attempt with a brawl that has Zeppo engaged in a fist fight, as Groucho plays fight announcer. The scene ends with Groucho pitching hay in the air and "looking for a needle in a haystack." It is a feeble fade-out, but the film provided a vehicle for enough Marx merriment to keep their reputation soaring.

Critic Mordaunt Hall wrote in *The New York Times* of August 8, 1931:

"The first morning of the Marx Brothers' latest shadow comedy took place yesterday about 10:30 at the Rivoli. Charlie Chaplin presented his *Gold Rush* several years ago at the Strand at midnight and proved that it is never too late to laugh, and now this quartet of clowns proves that they can stir up boisterous laughter virtually just after breakfast.

"This picture bears the title of *Monkey Business*, which considering everything, is quite apt. . . . Whether it is really as funny as *Animal Crackers* is a matter of opinion. Suffice it to say that few persons will be able to go to the Rivoli and keep a straight face."

The New Yorker noted: "The advantage of this picture does not lie so much in any superior novelties on the part of the Messrs. Marx as in the fact that this is a movie contrived directly for the screen and not a rehash of a libretto."*

The record now stood at two pictures based on Broadway hits, and one new original created out of the move to Hollywood. The challenge now was to find another script that would prove sufficiently strong, and for the next picture Bert Kalmar and Harry Ruby were given the writing assignment. Will Johnstone and Perelman also added their skills. Kalmar and Ruby provided musical numbers as well. Once again the pattern was anything but simple. It took the usual exhausting round of getting ideas down, and arguing about them in frenetic story conferences.

Groucho was a tough critic of new material, and the brothers would all want their say. Zeppo was increasingly agitated about not having enough to do, and Groucho was annoyed at Zeppo's being annoyed. After months of hard work, discussions, changes and the sweat of many brows, there was a new Marx Brothers script, *Horse Feathers*, in which they were installed on a college campus. Again, Herman Mankiewicz was producer and Norman McLeod director. Thelma Todd stayed, on too, playing a "college widow." Zeppo was cast as Groucho's son, romantically in-

*One historical casting note: The Marxes' father, Frenchie, was used as an extra in the film. It was the only film in which he appeared. He died on May 11, 1933.

*MONKEY BUSINESS (1931). "Captain" Groucho teaching Chico
his own form of geography*

volved with Todd and getting to
sing a syrupy ballad. True to form,
the comedy would be safely in the
hands of Groucho, Chico, and Harpo.

Horse Feathers, released in
1932, continued in the stylistic
tradition now firmly established by
the Marx Brothers on stage and on
film. Anarchy reigned supreme,
and what story existed was sub-
jugated to the comedy routines.
Groucho cuts a comically ridiculous figure as the fast-talking Professor Quincy Adams Wagstaff,
president of hapless Huxley

College, which has not had a winning football team since 1888. As
usual, Chico and Harpo are disrep-
utable characters who attach themselves to Groucho.

Right from the beginning,
Groucho, in his cap and gown,
shows his overriding contempt for
the academic life. Addressing the
faculty, he remarks, "As I look
over your eager faces, I can readily
understand why this college is flat
on its back." Naturally, this leads
him to sing "(Whatever It Is) I'm
Against It," and with the faculty
acting as his chorus, he is soon into

HORSE FEATHERS (1932). The boys take over
Professor Robert Greig's classroom.

another song with such insane lyrics as "I soon dispose of all those who put me on the pan/Like Shakespeare said to Nathan Hale, I always get my man." In the vein of Gilbert and Sullivan, of whose works Groucho was very fond, the professorial chorus chimes in with "He always gets his man."

Later, Groucho spots Zeppo, a perennial student, sitting in the auditorium with a girl perched on his lap. He puns: "Young lady, would you mind getting up so I could see the son rise?" The picture has a loose plot involving Groucho, Chico, and Harpo trying to recruit football players from a speakeasy to bolster the miserable Huxley team in the big game. Naturally, they pick on the wrong men, one of whom is played by colorful character actor Nat Pendleton. The film ends with a football scene that is a gem of slapstick, as well as a glorious satire on the sport.

This scene reaches new heights of insanity as the brothers, incongrously dressed in versions of gridiron uniforms, join the crucial game. Chico calls signals like "Hey diddle diddle, the cat and the fiddle, this time I think we go up the middle." Harpo attaches an elastic to the ball so that it will zoom right back after he throws it, and more effectively, he drops banana peels to bring down the pursuing opposing team. And how can one describe

adequately the sight of Harpo racing a chariot-like garbage cart with two horses down the football field? The scene is a forerunner of the horserace climax to *A Day at the Races*. It takes slapstick outdoors in a free way which points to other film possibilities.

Horse Feathers also contains the memorable password scene, with the bizarre exchange in which Chico tells Groucho that he can't enter the speakeasy without knowing the password. Chico: "I give you three guesses." He hints: "It's the name of a fish." Groucho: "Is it Mary?" Chico: "Ha ha, at's-a no fish!" Groucho: "She isn't? Well she drinks like one. Let me see, is it sturgeon?" Chico: "Ah, you crazy, Sturgeon, he's a doctor, cuts you open whenna you sick." And so on, until they miraculously arrive at "swordfish."

Kalmar and Ruby also provided the film with a forgettable song called "Everyone Says I Love You," which is repeated far too often in the film. Zeppo gets a chance to croon it to Thelma Todd, and while it might have merely seemed excess baggage in 1932, it became pure camp in the sixties and seventies revival showings. The strength of *Horse Feathers* lies in the antics of the brothers, the surrealistic quality of the dialogue, the satirical havoc wrought upon college life and the college football mania of the era. The film was a

HORSE FEATHERS (1932). Harpo displays his police badges.

new affirmation of the Marx brand of comedy.

Philip K. Scheuer greeted the picture in the *Los Angeles Times* with: "The current Marx comedy is the funniest talkie since the last Marx comedy, and the record it establishes is not likely to be disturbed until the next Marx comedy comes along. This is only Marxian logic." And in *The New York Times*, Mordaunt Hall again tempered his approval with a touch of condescension: "Groucho's characteristic corkscrew humor, Chico's distortions of English, and Harpo's pantomime aroused riotous laughter from those who packed the theater for this first performance. Some of the fun is even more reprehensible than the doings of these clowns in previous films, but there is no denying that their antics and their patter are helped along by originality and wit."

Perceptively, *The New Yorker* observed: " . . . These Marxes are very special; there is no one else like Groucho or Harpo on stage or screen, and probably there never will be. So familiar now is the sense of humor they arouse that the mere idea of their presence starts a laugh."

With *Horse Feathers*, the brothers made the cover of *Time* Magazine, an event which marked their high level of national recognition.

Duck Soup, their next film and their last for Paramount, looms as among the most important in their careers. It is a pivotal picture, which reveals the social satire of which they were capable, and seeing it again raises anew the question of why this avenue of expansion was closed to them. The picture is now a special favorite of Marx aficionados and for very good reason. It is surrealistic comedy which neatly blends barbs at government, charlatan officials, and diplomatic intrigue with the usual Marxian mayhem, and it was made at a time when its comments had relevance to the international scene in which Hitler was gathering power.

The comedy, which Groucho, in retrospect, called the best they made for Paramount, should have excited those shaping the film industry into recognizing new facets of the Marx talents. But despite their fame, the brothers were up against the same commercial dogmas others had to grapple with. *Duck Soup* went against the conventional desire for pictures with clear-cut story lines, the kind of film the public was being programmed to enjoy.

Satire has always been virtually a dirty word in Hollywood. Anything that smacks of intellectualism has been mostly shunned by executives who find "entertainment" a much more magical word. Therefore, one must take with a grain of salt the protestations that *Duck Soup* was

HORSE FEATHERS (1932). "What's the password?"

HORSE FEATHERS (1932). Chico and Groucho get amorous with "college widow" Thelma Todd.

meant only to be funny, and that it was merely a case of finding a new environment for the routines of the brothers, who just happened to do a comedy that spoofs sacred cows.

This is not to say that everything buffs now read into the film was planned that way. But surely the satirical events that take place in the mythical kingdom of Freedonia evolved from a combination of writing, directing, and acting that was blessed with an acute perspective on the world and its excesses. Groucho, nevertheless, credits director Leo McCarey with being responsible for the film becoming an anti-war satire.

Released in 1933, *Duck Soup* came at a very critical time for the Marxes. They had already completed four pictures for Paramount. They were enjoying prestige, success, and an enormous following. They had been signed to do a radio series. Inevitably there would be arguments about financial arrangements with the studio. Their old contract was drawing to an end and the need for negotiating a new

HORSE FEATHERS (1932). Chico and Harpo find an unusual way to escape their captors.

From top to bottom: Groucho, Zeppo, Harpo, Chico, and Gummo

The Marxes on radio

DUCK SOUP (1933). The magnificent Margaret Dumont as Mrs. Teasdale

1453-20

one was on the horizon. In fact, there had been a split before the making of *Duck Soup*. The Marx Brothers announced they were leaving Paramount and forming a new company with Sam Harris. But this didn't last. They returned to the Paramount fold to do *Duck Soup*.

The director whom the Marx Brothers had wanted for their new picture was McCarey. He had directed Laurel and Hardy in some of their best silent films, and was considered skillful at comedy and a creative filmmaker. McCarey didn't relish any such prospect at first because of the Marx reputation for being so difficult to manage. The stories about their endless disruptions and other evidence of potential chaos were enough to make a director balk.

But McCarey was enlisted, and there was the customary round of joint efforts to put together a script that would continue the brothers' success streak and solve the problem of the ever-demanding need for new material. Bert Kalmar and Harry Ruby came up with a screenplay again, as well as with music and lyrics, and Arthur Sheekman and Nat Perrin, by now old Marxian hands, added "additional dialogue."

Margaret Dumont was back again as the haughty foil, this time playing Mrs. Teasdale, the wealthy power-center who makes Groucho, otherwise known as Rufus T. Fire-fly, the dictator of Freedonia, which would never be in more trouble. A state welcome, complete with attractive girls and the singing of the national anthem ("Hail, Freedonia!"), is prepared, but Firefly is late. When he finally shows up, the banter between Groucho and Dumont is like old times:

Mrs. Teasdale: "The future of Freedonia rests on you. Promise me you'll follow in the footsteps of my husband." Firefly: "How do you like that? I haven't been on the job five minutes and already she's making advances to me. Not that I care, but where is your husband?" Mrs. Teasdale: "Why, he's dead." Firefly: "I'll bet he's just using that as an excuse." Mrs. Teasdale: "I was with him to the very end." Firefly: "Huh! No wonder he passed away." Mrs. Teasdale: "I held him in my arms and kissed him." Firefly: "Oh, I see. Then it was murder." Undaunted, Mrs. Teasdale tells Firefly, "This is a gala day for you." To which he replies, "That's plenty. I don't think I could handle more than a gal a day."

Before *Duck Soup* runs its merry course, there are plots and counter plots, and ultimately the breakout of war. Chico plays Chicolini and Harpo is Pinky, two highly inept spies for the rival power-seeker, suavely played by Louis Calhern. Character actor Edgar Kennedy, famed for his exasperated "slow

DUCK SOUP (1933). Mrs. Teasdale greets the new President of Freedonia.

*DUCK SOUP (1933). The world's most unlikely spies,
with Louis Calhern and Verna Hillie*

burn," is also on hand as the owner
of a lemonade stand who has an
hilarious encounter with Harpo.
Chico doubles as minister of war,
Harpo as Groucho's driver. Zeppo,
in what turned out to be his farewell
role, is Groucho's secretary.

A high point of the film is "The
Country's Going to War," a
production number satirizing how
patriotism is hysterically whipped
up among the populace to drive
people into war. The war itself is a
slapstick brawl, perhaps sym-
bolized by Harpo standing with a
sandwich sign bearing the slogan
"Join the Army and See the Navy."
Harpo also responds to Firefly's
urgent cry for help by posting a
"Help Wanted" sign outside their
besieged headquarters. Informed at
one point that he is shooting his
own men, Firefly says: "Here's five
dollars. Keep it under your hat.
Never mind. I'll keep it under my
hat." The film is riddled with im-
aginative sight gags, ranging from
Harpo on a Paul Revere-type ride
(*this* Paul Revere stops his ride at
the sight of a blonde in a window),
to the celebrated sequence in which
Harpo and Chico don Groucho dis-
guises and confront Groucho as if
he is looking in a mirror.

Duck Soup looked even better by
the 1970s, what with the protests
about the Vietnam war and the exposure of corruption in high places.

DUCK SOUP (1933). Chico and Groucho in a pensive mood

At the time it was released, it could be related to the rise of Hitler. (Marx Brothers films were banned in Germany because the Marxes were Jewish and the films were not shown there until after World War II.) *Duck Soup* received a lukewarm reception when released in 1933. Mordaunt Hall wrote in *The New York Times* that "this production is, for the most part, extremely noisy without being nearly as mirthful as their other films."

Critic John S. Cohen, Jr., claimed in the *New York Sun* that the Marx Brothers had taken "something of a nose dive" and that the film "just doesn't happen to be very amusing in comparison with their previous films" and also that "the satirical situations aren't interesting in themselves." Richard Watts, Jr., had a mixed opinion in the *Herald-Tribune*. While noting that the adventures in the film "are properly madcap and completely cockeyed and there is much in the work that is hilariously and crazily funny," he expressed the "fear that American experts at satirical farce are not at their best when mocking the frailties of dictatorship. Perhaps they are not bitter enough. Possibly they strive too desperately to retain their good disposition."

The film received a better reaction from Philip K. Scheuer in the *Los Angeles Times*: "Their latest melange ranges from the pun of burlesque to inspired satire on governmental pomp and circumstance. If it has not as consistently keen-edged wit as their earlier photographed stage plays, it is still more laughable than the output of any of their current competitors, and it ranks (if a Marx Brothers comedy can be ranked at all) perceptibly ahead of *Horse Feathers*."

Despite the appreciation of *Duck Soup* by many, the mixed notices left the Marxes in an uncomfortable situation with Paramount. Now their next contract would be negotiated against the background of a film that was not successful and the rule in Hollywood was that you were as good as your last picture. Unfortunately, instead of the Marxes being lauded for making a film that heightened the significance of their original style of humor, the pressure was on for them to avoid such identification. They wanted to discover how to achieve wider acclaim and larger box office grosses within the framework of a system that didn't put a high value on anarchy, however inspired.

There were also advantages to the direction in which they were heading, as anyone who has ever laughed through *A Night at the Opera* or *A Day at the Races* will attest. But never again were the brothers to display as much unbridled lunacy, free-form style, and satirical thrust that combined to

DUCK SOUP (1933). Fighting for Mrs. Teasdale's honor

make *Duck Soup* a film that has gathered stature as a comedy classic. This was a moment of truth, and had the Marx Brothers been able to continue making pictures more in the spirit of *Duck Soup*, they might have left us an even richer legacy and could even have grown as artists.

By 1946, Groucho was to lament in an interview with Mary Morris of *PM*: "The movies don't recognize any real heavies in the world. You don't dare make a joke that implies anything wrong with Franco. The poor public is smothered under tons of goo."

ROARING WITH THE LION

Actors, even when receiving accolades, can be insecure about their status. This can be even more true of comedians. The Marx Brothers had been on a filmmaking treadmill since leaving the stage, where they were basically most at home, and they now had to think carefully about where they would be going next. Their contract with Paramount was expiring against the background of a film greeted unenthusiastically. And all the Marxes' plans had to be formed against the larger background of a country still in the depths of the Depression.

Chico, forever on the lookout for new opportunities, struck up an acquaintance with Irving Thalberg, MGM's production head, at a card game. Many in the industry considered Thalberg a boy wonder with a magical touch and insight into how successful films should be made. He expressed interest in the brothers, and a chat at luncheon set the stage for the liaison that was to develop. Thalberg wasn't wild about *Duck Soup* and didn't see the Marxes as free-form comics or satirists. He was firmly oriented toward packaging a picture with a clear story line, and he believed that the Marx pictures should be structured so that the audience could be involved with the brothers as characters. He also thought that a love story was an essential ingredient.

Thalberg had ideas on how to harness the comic energy of the brothers into films that would be more popular and profitable. The brothers respected Thalberg for this, even though they had qualms about how their comedy and his concept would mix, but they went along with the approach. A deal was made with Thalberg at MGM, and the brothers signed to do two pictures with an arrangement that included a guarantee of 15 percent of the gross, which was unheard of in those days. Lingering doubts about their comedy getting lost in Thalberg's more complex film conceptions gave way to their regard for his astuteness, the deal they were able to make, and the need for going forward.

While the Marxes and Thalberg got along, the stories are legion about their needling him and playing Marxian pranks. Thalberg was well known for keeping people waiting. Once the Marxes are said to have set fire to papers stuffed at his door, so that the smoke crept through, and when he was forced to open the door, they swept into his office. They were also irritated by his habit of walking out of a meeting and not coming back for a long time, if at all. Once they

A NIGHT AT THE OPERA (1935). On the set with Groucho,
writer Al Boasberg, Kitty Carlisle, and director Sam Wood.
In the background: Walter Woolf King

moved furniture against his office
door so that he had trouble getting
back in. The most famous story is
that during one of these absences
they started a small fire in his office, and the scene which greeted
the returning Thalberg was the
Marx Brothers, completely naked
and roasting potatoes.

The first picture to be done
evolved into *A Night at the Opera*,
from an original story by James
Kevin McGuinness. Bert Kalmar
and Harry Ruby worked on a
script, then a few more writers tried
their hands. Groucho was unhappy
with the results, and he didn't have
much respect for other available
writers MGM might call upon from

what he considered a stable of
hacks. George S. Kaufman and
Morrie Ryskind had amply proved
their ability to write for the Marxes, and Thalberg, apparently at
Groucho's instigation, got them to
come in on this effort to top past
Marx films. Comedy writer Al
Boasberg was also among those
brought in on the project. Boasberg, a character whose larger-
than-life qualities became legend
among his colleagues, liked to
write funny material while soak-
ing in a bath. Wherever he chose to
create, he was highly regarded as a
gag man. To direct, Thalberg got
Sam Wood. According to Groucho, it wasn't because Thalberg

thought of him as a cinematic talent, but because Wood was subservient enough to take orders from Thalberg on how scenes should be done or reshot. Even without Thalberg's intervention, Wood liked to do each take about twenty to twenty-five times.

Thalberg recognized that there was some merit to the way the Marxes had honed their routines according to audience response. Their first two pictures had been based upon shows they had performed on stage. Therefore, it was decided that before filming began on *A Night at the Opera*, sequences would be tried out on tour. What we now see as some of the funniest Marx material in this uproarious film is the result of much trial and error. The stage show was called *Scenes from a Night at the Opera*,

and it toured Western cities. Ryskind, Kaufman, and Boasberg went along to do the reworking. Thalberg began dropping in on road stops to keep an eye on progress. For the first time in a Marx Brothers show, Zeppo was not on stage. Bowing to his long-simmering feeling of merely being an extra brother, he had given up. His future was to be as a Hollywood agent, not as a Marx Brothers adjunct.

Margaret Dumont, Siegfried Rumann, and Kitty Carlisle, all in the film, were not in the stage tryouts. Other performers went through the paces that were to be taken over by the stars. Allan Jones was present, however, as the romantic lead, a part that would formerly have been a Zeppo role.

On seeing the show in Salt Lake

A NIGHT AT THE OPERA (1935). Otis P. Driftwood and Mrs. Claypool

A NIGHT AT THE OPERA (1935). Kitty Carlisle comforts Harpo.

City, Harry L. Guss wrote in *Variety* of April 17, 1935: "A bit slow, its pacing potentialities for future speed and tempo are obvious." Guss singled out the contract-reading scene in which Groucho and Chico massacre legal language and destroy its pretensions, as "one of the best things in the show," and this became a highlight of the film. Eventually many ideas were worked through, and probably the most significant development was the evolution of the stateroom scene, which has become one of the best-loved sequences in film comedy.

Inevitably, there has been a dispute about who should get most credit for the scene. Groucho, ego flourishing as usual, lays claim to inspiring the bits and pieces that made it so hilarious. In the beginning the scene was written only for Groucho and Dumont, but it was expanded in tryout. By the time the scene was committed to film, many people were crowded into the tiny stateroom, including an army of ship's helpers, a woman looking for her Aunt Minnie, and, of course, Harpo honking his horn or blissfully sleeping through the pandemonium. It is excruciatingly funny, and it is the moment fans wait for now.

Thalberg got his wish to have a plot with a love story. Kitty Carlisle and Allan Jones play a couple in love but forced to separate, and also according to Thalberg precepts, it is up to the Marxes to help love triumph. Jones is a singer looking for a break, and the brothers must outmaneuver the rival of Jones and just about everyone else before Jones can get his opera contract. Margaret Dumont, the lovable foil, does wonderfully as Mrs. Claypool, the rich, society-oriented patron of the opera, and Sig Rumann as the impresario fumes and sputters at the impossibilty of dealing with Groucho as the conniving, fortune-hunting Otis B. Driftwood. Chico is another hustler, Fiorello, and Harpo is sidekick Tomasso. So much in the film belongs to the best of the Marx routines. The climactic scene in which they tear into an opera performance is the pinnacle of comedy, with the orchestra playing "Take Me Out to the Ball Game" instead of the overture to *Il Trovatore*, backdrops changing every minute, and Harpo defying gravity by scampering up the scenery. Earlier in the film, the impersonation of three bearded Russian aviators is also memorably side-splitting. Chico's speech to the crowd assembled at City Hall is one of his best examples of scrambled syntax and non sequiturs.

Thalberg succeeded in creating a film that had the glossy look of first-rate picture making. Giving the Marxes this kind of treatment reinforced their stature as major

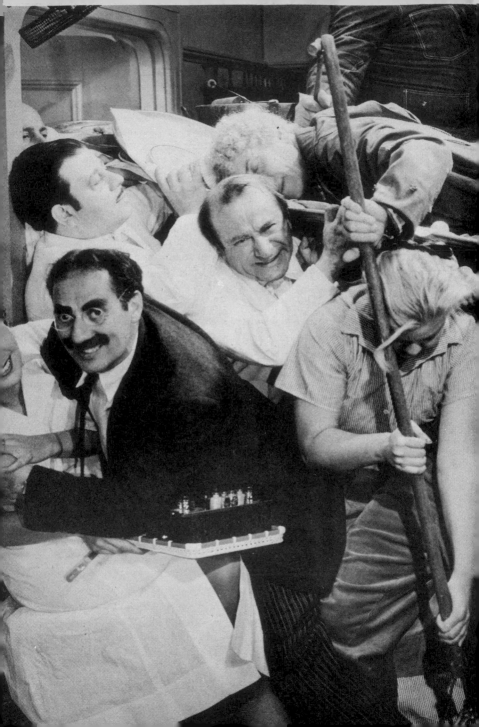

A NIGHT AT THE OPERA (1935). Pandemonium in a stateroom

A NIGHT AT THE OPERA (1935). Harpo, Chico, and Groucho, with Allan Jones and Sig Rumann

film stars. As for the idea of story, motivation, and audience identification being essential ingredients for the Marxes, there is strong evidence to question this. Most people who view *A Night at the Opera* wait impatiently for the singing to finish, the "love stuff" to disappear, and for the Marx Brothers to come back on screen in full command.

This was observed in a review by Andre Sennwald in *The New York Times*: "It would be pleasant to report that the omission of Zeppo, the romantic juvenile of the gang, also means the elimination of the conventional musical comedy romance. That isn't quite so, although the boys do keep the amorous business from becoming too tiresome." However, Sennwald was enthusiastic about the film. While judging it "a trifle below their best," he called it "the loudest and funniest screen comedy of the winter season" and noted that "the Marxist assault on grand opera makes a shambles of that comparatively sacred institution."

If the Marx Brothers were to be channeled away from their inspired anarchy into a more commercial strait jacket, for the moment, at least, they were in a stylish vehicle. The public took to it enthusiastically, although there was a shaky moment when the film was previewed before an audience in Long Beach, California. The response was deadly. Thalberg, bouncing back quickly, arranged for its showing in another theater in San Diego, and the reception was exhilarating. If Thalberg had run scared at the first reaction, as some producers do, he might have sent the film back to the editing room to be cut ruthlessly. But he stuck by his guns, had a hit, and the film grossed three million dollars.

Now what could be done for an MGM encore? The obvious answer was to come up with a new situation that paralleled the formula of *A Night at the Opera*. That was easier said than done. Some eighteen script versions were written before Thalberg was reasonably satisfied with *A Day at the Races*. Battles developed over writing credits, and who did exactly what was the subject of violent argument. The final screenplay credit went to George Seaton, Robert Pirosh, and **George Oppenheimer**. Al Boasberg also took part in the creation but asked that his name be taken off as a result of the credit dispute. George S. Kaufman was involved in the doctoring, but didn't want to take any script assignment. Pirosh and Seaton had been among those who helped in the making of *A Night at the Opera*; Oppenheimer was writing shows for the "Flywheel, Shyster, and Flywheel" radio series of the Marxes.

When recently asked what the hardest thing was in writing for the Marx Brothers, Oppenheimer, who subsequently became a drama critic, replied: "Writing for the Marx Brothers! Period! Groucho would drive me crazy. I like Groucho, but at 7:30 in the morning he might think something was great and later he'd want to change

A NIGHT AT THE OPERA (1935). Groucho breaks up a dinner for three Russian aviators.

A NIGHT AT THE OPERA (1935). The cast assembled

everything. Harpo was sweet. Chico was nothing. He'd only be interested in whether he had as many lines as Groucho. I've always hated writing for any comedians."

As with *A Night at the Opera*, Thalberg followed the pattern of trying the key ingredients out on a stage in various theaters. This time the cities chosen included Minneapolis, Duluth, Chicago, Cleveland, Pittsburgh, and San Francisco. Ideas and gags were tried and thrown away. Some of the better material was eliminated as well as efforts that didn't work. Groucho had a sure-fire song that audiences found hilarious. Called "Dr. Hackenbush" and written by Kalmar and Ruby, it was in the vein of the Captain Spaulding number. But it was eventually cut.

Nevertheless, the song is one of those treasures which Groucho has subsequently warbled off-screen. Many lines that started off as duds were altered slightly to trigger laughter. The brothers were old hands at finding the magic combination of words, inflection, mannerisms and timing.

With the results good enough on stage to inspire confidence that there could be a new winner, production began in Hollywood. It was barely under way when Thalberg, only thirty-seven years old, died unexpectedly of double pneumonia. The news was a thunderclap, and the event was one of those traumas that periodically come to Hollywood. The death of a man of Thalberg's stature in the prime of life suddenly makes everyone else aware of their own mortality. For the Marx Brothers it meant the loss of the man on whom they were pinning future hopes. What would happen to *A Day At the Races*?

Thalberg had so firmly placed his imprint on the project, that once recovered from the shock, his associates picked up the pieces and proceeded. As the filming went along there were rewrites and hesitations that may have arisen from a lack of Thalberg's confidence. Ambitious set ups were called for in the film. According to the *New York Post*, some six-thousand gallons of water were pumped into a 200 x 250-foot tank on one of the sound stages, which contained a set large enough for five hundred people. It was set up

for the elaborate water carnival production number that included lavish effects and a rising orchestra platform.

The finished product, while having its ragged moments, contains magnificent comedy. Groucho is in peak form as Dr. Hugo Z. Hackenbush, a horse doctor who arrives to take over an ailing sanitarium. He is introduced to his bearded colleagues who haughtily present their credentials: "John Hopkins, '17." "Mayo Brothers '28." Groucho responds, "Dodge Brothers, '29." He prescribes a golf-ball sized pill to rich patient Mrs. Emily Upjohn (the inimitable Margaret Dumont). When crooked business manager Whitmore (Leonard Ceeley) protests that it looks like a horse pill, the following priceless

On the set of A DAY AT THE RACES (1937)

A DAY AT THE RACES (1937). Groucho and Esther Muir

A DAY AT THE RACES (1937).   *"Sherlock Holmes"*
interrupts the liaison of Groucho and Esther Muir.

dialogue ensues.

Mrs. Upjohn: "Are you sure, doctor, you haven't made a mistake?" Groucho: "You have nothing to worry about. The last patient I gave one of those to won the Kentucky Derby." Whitmore: "Uh, may I examine this, please? Do you actually give those to your patients? Isn't that awfully large for a pill?" Groucho: "No, it was too small for a basketball and I didn't know what to do with it. Say, you're awfully large for a pill yourself."

Whitmore: "Doctor Wilmerding, just what is your opinion?" Wilmerding: "It must take a lot of water to swallow that." Groucho: "Nonsense, you can swallow that with five gallons." Whitmore: "Isn't that a lot of water for a patient to take?" Groucho: "Not if she has a bridge in her mouth. You see, the water flows under the bridge and the patient walks over the bridge and meets the pill on the other side."

The picture contains the memorable "Tutsi frutsi ice cream" scene in which Chico as Tony, the hustling sanitarium chauffeur, cons Groucho at the track-betting window by selling him a library of books for handicapping the horses. Slapstick reigns supreme when the brothers conduct what passes for a medical examination of Mrs. Upjohn in which Sig Rumann as expert Dr. Leonard X. Steinberg tries to expose Groucho as a fraud. (Steinberg: "She looks like the healthiest woman I ever met." Hackenbush: "You look like you never *met* a healthy woman!") The villain of the film is Douglass Dumbrille as Morgan, a racetrack owner who wants to take over the sanitarium and make it a casino. When sexy blonde siren Esther Muir is sent to seduce Groucho, the scene turns into chaotic comedy as the seductress becomes the target of two demented wallpaper-hangers named Chico and Harpo. The great wind-up is a horserace with Harpo as the world's most unlikely jockey who wins the race in a last-minute reversal, prompting a delirious Groucho to exclaim to Dumont, "Marry me, and I'll never look at another horse!"

The love interest Thalberg favored is provided here by Maureen O'Sullivan as Judy, owner of the endangered sanitarium, and Gil, played by Allan Jones, who invests all of their savings on a horse. The thin plot comes from the Marxes trying to help Judy save the sanitarium. Jones is given his chance to sing at the lavish water carnival, which also provides the opportunity for Chico to play the piano and Harpo to give his harp solo. Another musical interlude succumbs to racial stereotypes of the day, as Harpo and a crowd of blacks dance and sing "Who Dat Man?" which segues into the song

A DAY AT THE RACES (1937). A wary Groucho and two antic bellboys.

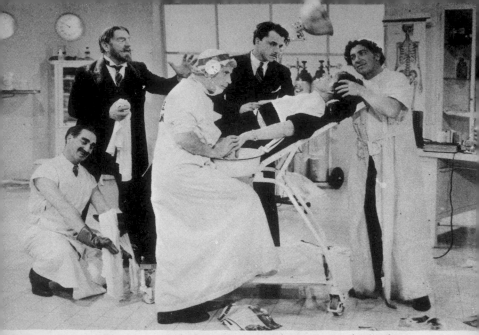

*A DAY AT THE RACES (1937). A medical examination
unique in medical history.
Horrified observers: Sigfried Rumann and Leonard Ceeley*

"All God's Chillun Got Rhythm."
Five thousand blacks in Los
Angeles auditioned for this musical
number. The dancers are brilliant
and featured singer Ivy Anderson is
outstanding, but the choral ren-
ditions and exaggerated movements
fit the racist pattern of the times.
Some of the critical comments
reflect the general insensitivity.
Variety talks of "a Harlemania
sequence with Harpo leading the
dusky cavalcade" and of the
blacks being "more or less dragged
in by their bojangles." This sequence has been cut for television
showing. NOT ON TCM

It is interesting to note how many
of the reviews of *A Day at the
Races* complained about saddling
the Marxes with too many ex-
traneous diversions. *The New York
Herald-Tribune* predicted that
Marx fans "are sure to be happy,"
but observed: "The plot is actually
taken seriously at times, which is all
wrong with a Marx Brothers picture." *The New York Times* called
the picture "comparatively bad
Marx" and while acknowledging
some comedy that works and giving
credit to the musical numbers, concluded: "Somehow, though, we like
to take our Marx Brothers straight,

A DAY AT THE RACES (1937). Harpo and friend

and they can't come too fast." The *London Times* was less agitated when the film opened in England, contending that "the little weak sentiment which trickles at intervals into the story is nothing but a faint interruption, and is forgotten as soon as it is over."

Director Sam Wood defended that approach to the film in an interview with the *World-Telegram*, contending: "There is as much, if not more, need for relief from mad comedy as from the starkest tragedy," and he prescribed romance and music as "the best forms for such rest periods."

Many disagreed with this point of view, but their criticism appeared to have little effect. The Marxes had begun to travel down the path which Thalberg had mapped out for them. There would definitely be no more pictures like *Duck Soup*.

Much has been written about the decline of the Marx Brothers in films, and there is stubborn disagreement about how weak or how funny this or that picture was after *A Night at the Opera* and *A Day at the Races*. Critics differ. The Marxes differed themselves, sometimes judging harshly films some critics found hilarious. But mostly there is a consensus that a downhill trend set in. The general diagnosis is failure to come up with fresh gag material, plots, and situations, and the resulting relegation of Marx pictures to hack work by the studios involved.

That is merely attempting to deal with the symptoms. The basic illness is traceable to two factors. One is the direction the Marxes went after *Duck Soup*. By choosing the Thalberg conception, they were abandoning the possibility of growing as comic artists. They could still be hilarious, but they were not pursuing projects that might have expanded their abilities and horizons. Instead, the questions always were: How can they be funnier than they were in the last picture? What can be done next to cash in on their talent and reputation?

The system of grinding out pictures for commercial rather than for artistic reasons had diverted the Marxes from their precious individuality, which no longer had a chance to expand as it did in the formative stages of their careers.

ONWARD AND DOWNWARD

Everything was reduced to holding on to what was already established. Had a more creative atmosphere flourished, the ensuing pictures might have been fresher.

The other problem was the sheer extent of public exposure. How many films can talented comedians make and still retain the same level of humor? The Marxes were their own worst competitors. Looking at some of the films that were panned proves this. Whatever faults *Room Service* may have, it is still exceedingly funny, particularly when compared with the comic fare one usually encounters. *The Big Store*, for all its detractors, has sequences that are creatively comic and the picture is a sure laugh-getter for audiences. Children, in particular, enjoy it. To acknowledge the merits of their lesser films is not to deny a sameness of their content. But had the Marxes been able to elaborate upon their individualism, they might have had a better chance to beat the pressure of overexposure. But they were not the first nor will they be the last artists to be used up by a business with little concern for art or the well-being of exceptionally talented people.

Given this combination of circumstances, there really was nowhere to go but down. And even after the brothers believed they should stop, based on their own attitudes and instincts, financial pressures and probably ego drove them to continue. Chico especially was forever in need of more money as a result of his incessant gambling losses. Groucho and Harpo were in better shape, and as impatient as they grew with Chico, they wanted to help him.

Their pictures completed on their MGM deal, Groucho, Chico and Harpo signed with RKO to star in *Room Service*. RKO had paid a record $225,000 for the film rights to the play, which had been a New York stage hit produced by George Abbott. The idea was to retailor the comedy as a Marx vehicle. The stage stars to be replaced were Sam Levene, Philip Loeb, and Teddy Hart. (Loeb eventually got a part other than the one he played on Broadway.) The story concerns a down-at-the-heels theatrical troupe, headed by Groucho as a shoestring producer. He is trying to avoid being thrown out of a hotel, while scrounging for money to do a first play by a rube author.

On screen the property becomes another framework for Marxist hustling and conning, defying authority, and raising general hell. Dependable Morrie Ryskind was given the job of adapting the play, and William A. Seiter, an active director since the early twenties, was given the unenviable task of guiding the Marxes. The film now has the added retrospective attraction of Lucille Ball and Ann Miller as the female leads. There aren't as many memorable Marx moments in this one, but most viewers recall Harpo's fiendish consumption of an enormous salad in seconds (he even catches a pinch of salt Chico has tossed over his shoulder) and his frantic pursuit of a live turkey which flies out of an open window. Harpo also shines in a scene as a bed-ridden patient who somehow cannot say "Ahhhh" to the doctor. He finally uses a squeaky kewpie doll under his pillow.

Room Service was the first film that was not created specifically for the Marx Brothers' talents. The idea of taking over parts that had been played by others was a gamble, and pre-release publicity made much of the departure. Chico said afterwards in a 1939 interview with Eileen Creelman in the *New York Sun:* "It was the first time we had tried doing a play we hadn't created ourselves. And we were no good. We can't do that. We've got to originate the characters and the situations ourselves. Then we can do them. Then they're us. If we get a gag that suits our characters we can work it out and make it ours. But we can't do gags or play characters that aren't ours. We tried it and we'll never do it again."

The reviews were surprisingly good. Archer Winsten wrote in the

*ROOM SERVICE (1938). With Harpo, Frank Albertson,
Groucho, Chico, and Lucille Ball*

*ROOM SERVICE (1938). Hapless Frank Albertson is given
"instant measles" by the Marxes.*

ROOM SERVICE (1938). Three startled Marx Brothers and Frank Albertson

New York Post: "On the stage it was a riot. On the screen it's still a riot, plus the Marx brothers." He described the ways in which the brothers couldn't make the most of the play's inherent qualities, but concluded: "Anyway, the lines and situations do stack up as the funniest among current movies." Rose Pelswick in the *New York Journal-American* called the picture "fast, loud and funny."

Frank S. Nugent commented in *The New York Times*: "While there may be some question about the play's being a perfect Marx vehicle, there can be none about its being a daffy show." *The New Yorker* summed it up: "As comic pictures go, this ranks certainly above average. . . . As Marx Brothers movies go, however, it is a minor effort."

Jesse Zunser observed in *Cue*: "*Room Service* is minus song, minus 'spectacle,' minus stagey musical interludes, but plus a script that is foolproof, gags that are dynamite for laughs, and comedy sequences that stop just this side of hysteria."

Next it was back to MGM. The Marxes went to work on what was one of their feeblest films, *At the Circus*. Without Thalberg, the magic for them was gone at the

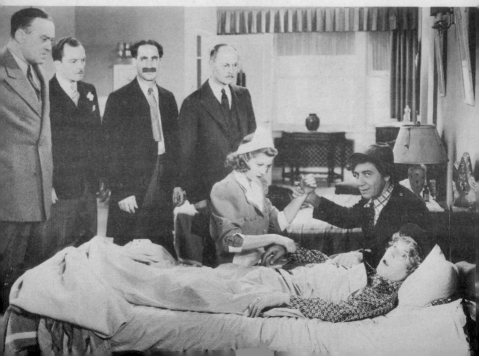

ROOM SERVICE (1938). Harpo takes his turn at feigning illness for the hotel management.

AT THE CIRCUS (1939). Harpo roars back at a lion.

studio. Now the producer was Mervyn LeRoy, and the frustrating job of trying to rig a screenplay that would provide a funny enough backdrop went to Irving Brecher, and Edward Buzzell, a stage actor who had turned to directing in the early thirties, was given a crack at handling the Marxes. The brothers battled to be permitted to have their customary road tour, but MGM was in a hurry to get the film made.

One good item in the film was the number "Lydia, the Tattooed Lady," by Harold Arlen and E. Y. Harburg, rendered by Groucho in his inimitable nasal tones. The supporting performers are entertaining—Eve Arden as a trapeze artist with whom Groucho shares a funny scene, Nat Pendleton as the circus strong man, and Margaret Dumont back as Mrs. Dukesbury after her absence from *Room Service*. Once again she is amorously pursued by Groucho who recalls a liaison they never had. ("We were young, gay, reckless. That night I drank champagne from your slipper. Two quarts. It would have been more, but you were wearing inner soles.") The romantic interest is provided by Florence Rice and Kenny Baker, the latter trying to come up with money to save the circus. It's the old business of the

101

AT THE CIRCUS (1939). J. Cheever Loophole and Antonio Pirelli

Marxes having to lend a helping hand, but the gimmick grows weaker.

Groucho, as lawyer J. Cheever Loophole, has his customary assortment of gags and he and Chico are funny in their encounter with a midget. There is also a far-out climax featuring the Marxes, Margaret Dumont, and a gorilla on a trapeze. A line considered bold for the time in view of the censorship that prevailed was Groucho's aside to the audience after Eve Arden stashes a wallet in her bosom: "There must be some way I can get that wallet without getting into trouble with the Hays office." The picture does have its share of laughs, but there is a lethargic air to the whole project.

The reviews were largely unfavorable. "Passages of high hilarity, but there is no sustained comic note in their new offering," said the *New York Herald-Tribune*, while William Boehnel in *The World-Telegram* complained that "the film is done so sketchily that most of it is a series of blackouts ending on a punchline which nine times out of ten lacks a wallop." Frank Nugent in *The New York Times* viewed it as "a matter of more perspiration than inspiration" and Jesse Zunser warned in *Cue* that the Marxes "are in danger of coming a cropper soon unless they tumble into brighter material than their current limping vehicle."

Work began at MGM on creating another film, *Go West*. The job of writing the script fell again to Irving Brecher, with Edward Buzzell directing. The project kept getting postponed. Groucho wrote to his son, Arthur, "*Go West* has again been postponed. I don't know why the studio doesn't come right out and say they are afraid to make it. All I hear from the studio is an announcement once a week that I should come to the wardrobe department and be fitted for a pair of early American pants. My attitude is, take the money and to hell with them. I had my hair darkened about three weeks ago, to match my grease-paint mustache, but it has been so long since we were scheduled to start that the dye has faded and I will have to go and have it done all over again. So you see my theatrical career has dwindled down to being fitted once a week for a pair of early American pants and having my hair dyed every three weeks. This is a fine comedown for a man who used to be the toast of Broadway."[*]

Go West shows clear signs of strain, with everyone obviously having been hard pressed to find a way to turn the Marx Brothers loose on the Wild West. Reactions depend on how easily one laughs at the performers. The film begins

*Arthur Marx, *Life With Groucho* (New York: Simon and Schuster 1954), p. 232.

AT THE CIRCUS (1939). Groucho with Eve Arden

GO WEST (1940). Two con men, hard at work on Groucho

well, with a clever scene in a railroad station in which Chico and Harpo fleece Groucho, who this time is tagged with the moniker S. Quentin Quale. Chico has a string attached to a ten dollar bill, and he yanks it back each time Groucho pockets it. When Groucho won't let the bill out of his pocket, Harpo produces a scissors and cuts away Groucho's pants, including the pocket. "You know," Groucho remarks, "it's suddenly gotten very chilly in here." Other reasonably amusing scenes include Groucho's meeting with a drunken cowpoke ("Didn't we meet at Monte Carlo the night you blew your brains out?"), and Harpo's fight with the

villainous Red Baxter in which a whisk broom becomes a deadly weapon.

There is one gem of a sequence in the film, and it ranks among the best in all their pictures. It is an elaborate chase aboard a train, strongly reminiscent of Buster Keaton's chase in *The General*. To keep the engine puffing along, Harpo dismantles the wooden cars to provide firewood to keep the train going. Along the way, he tries to use popcorn for fuel and even serves as a human link between disconnected cars.

The Western spoof was greeted with much better reviews than *At the Circus*, although not in *The*

GO WEST (1940). A "dry" Harpo gapes at a beer-drinker,
while Chico looks on.

New York Times. Thomas M. Pryor liked neither the gags nor the story premise, and while he lauded the train chase, said in his review: "At a time when the national funnybone can stand some vigorous tickling, it is doubly disappointing to discover that the Marx Brothers are not nearly so comical in their new show." Other reviews were more favorable, with the *New York World-Telegram* asserting that the comedy "is about as good entertainment as you will find anywhere these days."

Although *Go West* did better critically than *At the Circus*, the problem still persisted of having to stand comparison with their past films each time out. The Marx Brothers themselves were growing tired of it all. There was a desperate need to breathe new life into their ventures, and rumors were already afloat that their next film, *The Big Store*, would be the last. Would it be an uproarious, happy exit, or a sad farewell?

This time the credits behind the camera were new. Charles Riesner was assigned to direct, and three writers—Sid Kuller, Hal Fimberg and Ray Golden—were credited with the screenplay from a story by Nat Perrin. For this outing the brothers are sent rampaging

GO WEST (1940). Happy Harpo, out West

THE BIG STORE (1941). Wolf J. Flywheel gets a warm reception from the store employees.

THE BIG STORE (1941). Groucho and Chico toast Margaret Dumont.

through a department store, with the customary dose of duplicity afoot. It remains for Groucho as master detective Wolf J. Flywheel to get to the bottom of it all. Margaret Dumont is again called upon to give the film class as the department store heiress who hires Groucho to protect her endangered nephew, played by Tony Martin. The villain is played with comic elan by Douglass Dumbrille. Virginia Grey is the subject of Martin's affections.

Much of the best humor in the film is supplied by Harpo, who is his usual droll self, whether using a portable fire hydrant to force other cars to move so he can park, operating a typewriter that sounds like a riveting machine, or playing the harp, the bass, and the violin in a delightful musical sequence. There are exquisite sight gags, including Harpo borrowing part of a shopper's dress and offering it back as matching material for a hat, leaving her with an exposed rear. Groucho, of course, gets his chance to woo Margaret Dumont in his familiar manner. Groucho: "There are many bonds that will hold us together through eternity." Dumont: "Really, Wolf? What are they?" Groucho: "Your government bonds, your savings bonds, your Liberty bonds."

There are enough props around the store for a myriad of gags, and the final chase on roller skates and bicycles is guaranteed to produce guffaws. An extremely funny musical sequence features singer Virginia O'Brien as a deadpan delight, but another musical interlude with Tony Martin singing "The Tenement Symphony" is now so corny it gets unintended laughs.

Reviews were very mixed when the film opened in the summer of 1941. The *New York Herald Tribune* thought that the picture had its ups and downs, "but more often holding to a straight course of merriment." Many reviewers complained that the film offered little or nothing that the Marxes had not used over the last two decades and felt that, despite a few fleeting moments of fun, the film was a severe disappointment.

Other reviews were kinder. The *New York Post* said ". . . their swan song is a laugh fest . . . not quite their merriest, but it is brighter than at least a couple of more recent ones." Theodore Strauss in *The New York Times* took note of the weak spots but held that "the boys are still the most erratic maniacs this side of bars . . . In short, *The Big Store* is of an old Marx Brothers design. But as the last remnant on the counter it's a bargain."

Those who include *The Big Store* as among the worst of Marx films have done it an injustice. The film holds up in many ways, and it would not have been an unworthy finale. But it wasn't the finale, despite the announcement that the Marxes were retiring.

Even before the release of *The Big Store*, Groucho issued a statement confirming retirement reports: "When I say we're sick of movies, what I mean is that people are about to get sick of us. By getting out now we're just anticipating public demand and by a very short margin. Our stuff is stale. So are we."

Careers die hard. There is always the lure of making a comeback, and there are usually financial pressures that make picking up more cash tempting. There is also the conflict within the performer. A lifetime of thriving upon applause, and in the comedian's sense, laughs, can leave a void.

The brothers were not totally idle. Harpo did a cameo appearance in the film *Stage Door Canteen*, released in 1943. Chico got a band together and performed in nightclubs. Groucho was building an independent reputation on radio. But the temptation of trying another picture had not been totally laid to rest.

A script called *A Night in Casablanca* offered a new possibility, and the idea seemed like a natural on the heels of the Warner Brothers hit *Casablanca*, starring Humphrey Bogart. One could

THE BIG STORE (1941). Groucho with Douglass Dumbrille and Margaret Dumont

THE BIG STORE (1941). Cornered by a cop

laugh merely thinking about the parody. But Jack and Harry Warner didn't laugh. They bristled at the use of the title, and tried to stop it. The occasion spawned one of Groucho's better-known letters, a masterful put-down. To Jack, he said that there had been other Jacks before him, notably Jack the Ripper and Jack and the Beanstalk. He reminded Harry Warner of "Lighthouse Harry of Revolutionary fame and a Harry Applebaum who lived on the corner of 93rd and Lexington." And assuring Warners that people who see his film could tell the difference between Harpo and Ingrid Bergman, he asserted:

"What about 'Warner Brothers'? Do you own that, too? You probably have the right to use the name Warner, but what about Brothers? Professionally, we were brothers before you were." In the face of such "logic" and other similar correspondence, legal problems faded away.

The Marxes formed a company with David L. Loew to produce the film, which was released by United Artists. The original screenplay was by Joseph Fields and Roland Kibbee, with Frank Tashlin providing additional material, as well as some substitute material. The idea afforded natural satirical opportunity, and putting the Marxes in the Casablanca atmosphere worked to some extent.

Again, the best material in the film goes to Harpo. He gets to engage in a wild duel in which he munches an apple while parrying every blow, performs a splendid charade to warn of impending danger for Groucho, and even takes over the controls of an airplane with childish glee. The film also has one of Harpo's best-known sight gags. He is leaning against a house, and a cop chastises him with the line, "Say, what do you think you're doing, holding up the building?" When he drags Harpo away, the inevitable happens. James Agee wrote in the *Nation*: "I think this is his best performance. Of the three he shows his age most. He is sadder than before, more acid, more subtle; he looks uncannily like Charlie Chaplin out of character."

Groucho's foil this time is Rumanian actress Lisette Verea, a far cry from the imperious Margaret Dumont, who had retired temporarily. (Verea: "I'm Beatrice Rheiner. I stop at the hotel." Groucho: "I'm Ronald Kornblow. I stop at nothing.") Sig Rumann, the Marxes' marvelous adversary in several films, is on hand as Nazi sadist Heinrich Stubel, posing as a Count Pfefferman who is trying to gain control of a hotel in which a cache of valuable art is hidden. He has been making a habit of systematically murdering the hotel's managers and Groucho is his latest target.

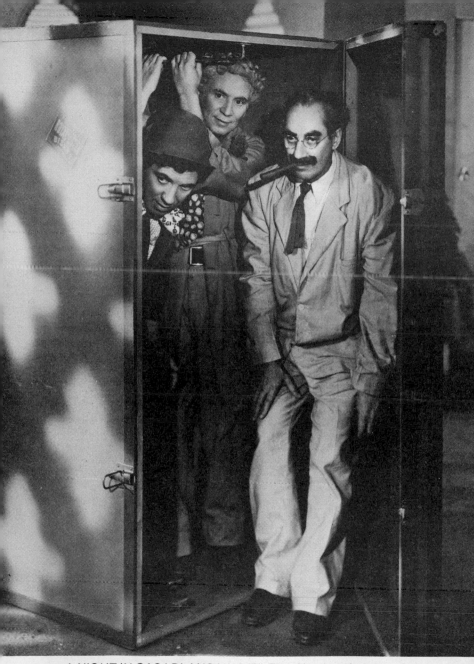

A NIGHT IN CASABLANCA (1946). Three in a wardrobe truck

A NIGHT IN CASABLANCA (1946). Three on a breadstick

Harpo in a quiet mood

James Agee, who looked upon Groucho as "the funniest satirist of the century," wrote in his *Nation* review: "Apparently you never know when you are seeing the last of the Marx Brothers; so it is unnecessary to urge anyone who has ever enjoyed them to see *A Night in Casablanca*. It is also beside the main point to add that it isn't one of their best movies for the worst they might ever make would be better worth seeing than most other things I can think of."

Time Magazine wrote: "Many things in *A Night in Casablanca* are not as funny as they should be—the Brothers have been doing this sort of thing for more than two decades, and are far too intelligent not to show the Marx of it; and the teetering hauteur of Margaret Dumont is especially missed. But even in their sleep the Marx Brothers could stage a funnier masque of anarchy than anyone else."

Whatever the favorable comments, there was a common agreement that the level was lower than ever, and it was again a question of matching previous success. *A Night in Casablanca* hardly ranks among their funniest films.

But this was not to be the Marxes' finale either. Groucho appeared on his own in an utter disaster, *Copacabana*, which is only occasionally redeemed by some of the wisecracks of Groucho, who plays a seedy agent, Lionel Devereaux, and also by Carmen Miranda as a flamboyant singer with whom Devereaux is involved. The plot creaks, and watching singer Andy Russell play himself is good for a few special groans.

Groucho can still get a laugh with a simple piece of business such as banging a clock on the wall when it stops working. A man in another room shouts: "What's the idea of waking people up at three o'clock in the morning." Groucho: "Three o'clock? Thanks."

But nothing helps. The film is just mostly dreadful, a weak plug for the old Copacabana night club in New York. Bosley Crowther in *The New York Times* called it a "hand-me-down musical frolic" and missed the other Marxes, whose help was desperately needed.

By 1949 Groucho, Chico, and Harpo were together again, making *Love Happy*. Groucho recalls its genesis as follows in *The Marx Bros. Scrapbook*: "Harpo had an idea that he was Charlie Chaplin and wanted to do a film by himself. But Chico needed money as usual so he got into it. I think the story was Harpo's idea. Before you know it they discovered that they couldn't finance the film unless all the Marx brothers were in it. The banks wouldn't put up the money and that's how I ended up in the film."*

*Groucho Marx and Richard J. Anobile, *The Marx Bros. Scrapbook* (New York: Grosset & Dunlap, 1974), p. 251.

COPACABANA (1947). Carmen Miranda
clearly disapproves of Groucho.

The picture is stolen by Harpo. One views it with appreciation for Harpo's lovable ways, and also with a twinge of regret. Harpo's excellence raises the question of whether there were untapped aspects of his talent which might have flourished in ways other than those in which he excelled as part of the Marx team. He has some marvelous sequences in *Love Happy*, including one in which he is victimized in comic fashion by a series of tortures inflicted by Ilona Massey as the scheming Madame Egilichi, desperate to get her hands on the missing Romanoff diamonds.

In an elaborate rooftop chase Harpo cavorts amid advertising billboards, and he also gets to use his famous coat that holds a seemingly endless inventory. Chico has relatively little to do, Groucho even less. As private eye Sam Grunion, Groucho is merely used as a "wrap-around" narrator of the story.*

During the production the financing was running out and the producer helped raise additional funds by making deals with companies for their names to be advertised on the signs in the Harpo-on-the-rooftops portion. When released in New York in April, 1950, Thomas M. Pryor of *The New York Times* called the film a see-saw affair and said: "Sometimes

*The film has Marilyn Monroe in one of her earliest screen appearances as a beauty who impresses Groucho with her undulating walk.

COPACABANA (1947). Groucho and the cowgirls

LOVE HAPPY (1949). With Otto Waldis and Marilyn Monroe

the antics are incredibly funny, and—pianissimo, please — sometimes the gags fall with a flat thud." The *New York Herald-Tribune* was more upbeat: "Marx fans will get their money's worth. An aficionado asks only for certain time-tested maneuvers from the comedians. They will get them at the Criterion."

The picture is weak by Marx standards, but there is joy in seeing some reminders of old glories, and the showcase for Harpo is welcome each time the film is viewed. His

harp solo is one of the loveliest in all his films.

The film marked the end of their joint appearances—almost. Groucho, Harpo, and Chico turned up briefly in a disastrous picture, *The Story of Mankind*, released in 1957. Based loosely, very loosely, on the Hendrik Willem van Loon book, it was produced, co-scripted, and directed for Warner Brothers by Irwin Allen, who later achieved fame with such films as *The Towering Inferno*. *The New York Times* called it a "protracted and tedious lesson in history that is lacking in punch, sophistication and a consistent point of view." Groucho played Peter Minuit, Harpo Isaac Newton, and Chico a monk. The brothers also came together again on television in *The Great Jewel Robbery*, and while it was moderately amusing for TV, it was pale stuff in the context of their careers.

Independently, Groucho had a cameo role in *Mr. Music* (1950), a Paramount musical starring Bing Crosby. For the record, and there is little other reason to mention it, Groucho played Emil J. Keck, the hero's sidekick in RKO's *Double Dynamite* (1951) starring Frank Sinatra and Jane Russell; and he played a sailor teamed with William Bendix and Marie Wilson in *A Girl in Every Port* (1952), an RKO comedy about horseracing.

The downward spiral of the Marx Brothers' careers fortunately has not obscured the heights to which they climbed when at their best. They enjoyed international acclaim, whether winning over the reluctant British, who were somewhat cool at first to their shenanigans, or whether Harpo was performing his pantomime on stage for the Russians. They were the toast of Hollywood and New York, and although their background was the low comedy of vaudeville, they became the favorites of leading

LOVE HAPPY (1949). Harpo and his captors: Bruce Gordon, Raymond Burr, Ilona Massey, and Melville Cooper

MR. MUSIC (1950).
With Bing Crosby

lights in the intellectual world.

The new generation shows no signs of allowing the Marxes to fade away. To the contrary, revivals of their films are still an event, and each picture is repeatedly analyzed for elements that the Marxes themselves didn't know were there. Books and articles about them are abundant, and even the scripts for their films are being published. The seventies have seen a veritable Marxomania.

Of the brothers, Groucho is the one who survived best in terms of a professional career on his own. His verbal gifts, wit, and the ability to make the most of his reputation

have served him well. A major contributing factor was the success of his long-running quiz show "You Bet Your Life," first on radio and then on television. His program struck the right chord. Groucho would playfully heckle his guests before they received a chance at the prize money. It was the perfect formula for him to make use of his ability to make sport of people without demolishing them and even to pay them comic compliments.

To a pretty nurse on one program, he said: "Why don't I ever get a nurse like you? The kind I always get make me yearn for the anesthetist." As for the questions,

DOUBLE DYNAMITE (1951). Groucho, Frank Sinatra, and Jane Russell pose for a photograph.

A GIRL IN EVERY PORT (1952). With William Bendix and Marie Wilson

they were often shams designed for the contestant to walk away with some money. A typical one would be "In what sport do you use a tennis ball?" Even contestants who had failed abysmally were given prizes for answering the question, "Who is buried in Grant's Tomb?"

Amazingly, when the shows were syndicated recently under the title "The Best of Groucho," they became a hit all over again. They caught on anew both with those who remembered them and with first-time viewers. Contestants on the show gained new prominence in their respective cities. Instead of the show being dated, the programs fit neatly into the trend toward nostalgia. "I'm a bigger star than I was thirty years ago," crowed Groucho.

The revival was a fitting capstone to Groucho's desire to succeed on radio and television. That was a longing he often spoke about, in addition to his aspirations as a writer. These were fulfilled through his books and articles, as well as several plays and scenarios. With Norman Krasna he co-authored the play *Time for Elizabeth*, which had a brief run on Broadway in 1948. He also teamed with Krasna for the well-received film *The King and the Chorus Girl*, which was released by Warner Brothers in 1937 and starred Fernand Gravet, Joan Blondell, Edward Everett Horton, Alan Mowbray, and Jane Wyman.

The revival of interest in Marx Brothers films enhanced Groucho's role as a later-life celebrity, and he gave special performances culled from his stage and film material and personal experiences. The award at the Cannes Film Festival thrust him into the limelight, and following suit with a belated special honor was the Motion Picture Academy. Groucho flew to New York to attend performances of *Minnie's Boys*, the Broadway musical about the Marx Brothers, the book of which was co-authored by his son Arthur, and he was besieged by autograph hunters.

"Could I have two signatures?," asked one fan. "I have two children and I couldn't possibly give one an autograph and not the other."

"You might try," Groucho growled jokingly, while obliging.

Chico's public appearances as the films phased out were primarily in night clubs. In 1956 he starred in a road company of *The Fifth Season*, playing the role originated on Broadway by comedian Menasha Skulnik. In his latter years he was too ill to work. Financial woes continued to plague him, and his brothers, although disgusted with his perpetual inability to handle money without gambling it away, looked after him and kept coming to the rescue.

Chico died on October 11, 1961 at seventy-four. Arthur Marx in *Son of Groucho* reflected: "Father had

Groucho on "You Bet Your Life" in 1953

Groucho on the set of THE WAY WE WERE (1973)
with Barbra Streisand

SKIDOO! (1968). Groucho with Alexandra Hay

always predicted that Chico's life would probably come to an end in bed—but out of shotgun wounds, not angina pectoris; and not in his own bed, but in some other husband's." The death of Chico ended all hopes that somehow, somewhere, the Marx Brothers could come together for one last film.

Harpo, also suffering from heart trouble, underwent open-heart surgery in 1964, and died at the age of seventy-five on September 28 of that year. He had decreed that he be cremated, with no funeral service of any kind. The experience at his brother Chico's funeral had been

enough for him. Three children, wearing Harpo wigs, had been posed in front of Chico's open casket in a publicity-seeking maneuver. A rabbi who had never known Chico gave the eulogy.

Zeppo, once having left the team, established what became a leading talent agency. Among his clients were Clark Gable, Carole Lombard, Robert Taylor, Fred Mac-Murray, and Barbara Stanwyck. In the beginning he handled deals for his brothers, but there were differences and frictions. Gummo, who went into a dress manufacturing business in New York, later moved to the West Coast and joined Zeppo in the agency, which was ultimately sold to MCA.

Zeppo continued to pursue his business interests, which have included racing thoroughbred horses, manufacturing a special type of gasket bought by an aircraft company, and in later life, patenting a special wristwatch for monitoring the functioning of the heart. Both Zeppo and Gummo are retired, each with a home in Palm Springs, California.

An intimate portrait of the brothers at a moment in later life is to be found in Arthur Marx's description of Harpo and Groucho hashing over Chico's life on the return ride from Chico's funeral. Disgusted at what they regarded as a hypocritical service, they indulged in what amounted to a roast of Chico. Harpo agreed that Groucho should have given the eulogy. "At least I wouldn't have been hypocritical," Groucho said. "They'd have known what Chic was really like when I got through with him."

IMMORTALITY

The effects of Marx Brothers film comedy are so far-reaching that a full measurement may not be possible. For example, there is evidence that the Marxes may have had a profound influence on the Theater of the Absurd. Playwright Eugene Ionesco once told an audience that the Marx Brothers had been one of the major influences on his work. Thus an important body of theatrical work bears a relationship to the liberated, anarchistic comedy of the Marxes. Their films have achieved a durability in themselves, but also a longevity through their influence on the art of others.

What is there about the pictures that these immensely funny fellows made which possessed the rare quality of durability? To say the films are funny is merely to beg the question, although just being funny is in itself an accomplishment. The ability to amuse even one generation is not something to be taken lightly. The Marx Brothers phenomenon begins with their unique talent as a trio of expert laugh-getters, deft and razor-sharp in their timing, and possessing a sense of what audiences respond to. They also know how to go about milking that response and have the ability to turn their knack for the ridiculous into tangible routines.

Surely one element in pleasing successive generations is universality. It is a worthwhile, fascinating experience to be in another country and watch a Marx comedy. The audience may not understand the language. The subtitles may not begin to accurately convey the gags. The translations barely suggest the flavor and the fervor of what is transpiring. But those images! Groucho, Chico, and Harpo are quickly recognized as a threesome bent on turning everything they encounter upside down. This wins an audience to their side. Their sight gags handily transcend the language barriers. Who cannot understand an over-populated stateroom cabin, the inexhaustible inventory spilling from Harpo's clothing, a leering little man with a painted mustache playing up to a haughty society matron, utter havoc on a football field, or the lunatic act of dismantling a wooden train to fuel an engine?

The very fact that Harpo does not speak establishes language-transcending comic potential. Harpo, through charades and use of his horn, talks to everyone. Alexander Woollcott was right. Harpo is one of the world's great clowns, a true artist. Coupling the playing of a harp with his comedy reinforces his international appeal, and the delicacy of his playing adds to the universal endearment.

Anarchy and rebellion are other ingredients which keep the Marx

Groucho and Chico in MONKEY BUSINESS (1931)

Brothers eternally fresh. With the battle between man and authority always raging everywhere in the world, the Marx Brothers can seem like a fresh wind of change in any era in which humor is subjected to outright censorship or subtle pressures toward conformity. Even the form of humor itself can be in danger, not from censors, but from commercial demands.

On television we see situation comedies becoming deadly with repetition, their mechanical canned laughter and rigid formats negating any resemblance to reality. When a program like "Laugh-In" comes along, its anarchy is a novelty. But then, in the pressure-cooker of doing shows week after week, even such an original program gets too structured, and the material turns stale. How invigorating it can be to flip the television dial to a channel broadcasting an early Marx Brothers film. Even in the confines of the small box, it is uplifting to see the brothers cavorting and thumbing their noses at the world.

This anarchy appeals to successive generations and to people in various societies. In a period of

133

The one . . . the only . . . Groucho!

Chico and daughter Maxine in 1935

repression or tension, a Marx Brothers film offers relief. In a period of free thought and political renaissance, the antics of the Marxes underscore, illustrate, and reinforce the prevailing mood.

Young people are particularly receptive audiences. It begins with childhood. Taking a child to see a Marx Brothers picture can be an unforgettable experience. You watch the youngster respond to the same antics that made you laugh. You leave the theater and the replay begins: "Remember the part when the guy with the mustache . . ." "Remember when he blows the horn to say something . . ." Most likely the youngster will want to see more Marx films and even go back to the same ones again and again. It seems safe to say that one day he or she will be bringing members of another generation to the films for their introduction. The whole life pattern for children is an endless set of rules. How natural that they would respond to watching Groucho, Chico, and Harpo making mincemeat of anything that smacks of law or order.

Later in life there is intellectual appreciation for the anarchistic, anti-establishment content in Marxian comedy. Generations who may be breaking out of a mold, or longing to do so, find special joy in these films. The attraction may be the gratifying sight of Groucho pummeling high society, especially his insults at haughty, socially prominent Margaret Dumont or, in *A Day at the Races*, making the medical establishment look ridiculous as Groucho, the horse doctor, rules the day. The law? Forget it. Cops are no match for the brothers. Higher education? All professors are stuffy idiots ready to acquiesce to any suggestion. Harpo making a funny face, or as he would put it, throwing one of his Gookies, makes short shrift of anyone in authority. Such antics and comic juxtapositions can be found in virtually all of the films. Anything resembling status quo is fair game.

This quality has been a unifying thread running through great comedy. Chaplin was the little tramp, inspiring sympathy when he came up against the bullies, oafs, and fools of the existing social order. W. C. Fields was also badgered by society and he fought back with muttered oaths and an ill-concealed contempt for the usual pillars of civilization, such as children, wives, or dogs. Buster Keaton battled the overwhelming natural forces of his surroundings. Harold Lloyd was boundlessly cheerful and optimistic while disaster lurked around every corner. It is possible to go too far in structuring everything into theory, but it is basic that much comedy, silent or verbal, relies on puncturing the pompous and defying a world geared to the destruction or

Harpo registers total disgust.

Harpo, recovered, plays his harp.

Margaret Dumont

at least the humiliation of its inhabitants.

The painful truth is that there has been a decline of comedy in films from the heyday of the silent era, and this paucity has set the stage for rediscovery of past comic genius. Much has been written about the reasons for the decline and fall of comedy. During the silent era, a premium was placed on inventiveness. But talkies switched the stress from creative sight gags to reliance on dialogue, and much was lost even while new potential was gained. The kind of opportunities the Marxes had in vaudeville for developing into stars has disappeared. It is necessary for would-be comedians to find new training ground, such as small nightclubs, coffee houses, or lecture circuits. The problem is that bookers want mainly ready-made stars, not trainees.

The most successful practioners of the sixties and seventies have understood how to blend gags and action, satire and lunacy. Woody Allen emerged as a cerebral film wit, able to spoof society and the characters floundering within society. But he also learned from the silent heritage, and his films draw broadly upon the slapstick tradition. Mel Brooks is far less cerebral in his films, but he can be magnificently liberated, and portions of *Blazing Saddles* are reminiscent of the unfettered antics of Marx

Brothers pictures. But despite the emergence of some important new talent, there has been an inadequate supply of comedy to satiate the public's appetite for laughter. Reliving the past is one answer.

Against this background the Marx Brothers keep re-emerging as remarkably skillful. Their superb slapstick and horseplay are delivered in a free form, with multiple levels from which diverse audiences can find amusement on individual terms. The range is from simple slapstick to satirical demolition of the social order. There has been no other combination remotely like them, and because their training ground no longer exists, there are not likely to be any comedians like them in the future.

Laurel and Hardy, unique in their way, exemplified a humor more limited in scope. This is not to belittle them, but their comedy did not have the depth of Marx comedy. Certainly one cannot compare Dean Martin and Jerry Lewis as a team with the Marxes. The Three Stooges? Merely roughhouse slapstick, and extremely repetitive. The Ritz Brothers, steeped in Borscht Belt humor, had their moments and perhaps bear re-discovery, but they can hardly be mentioned in the same breath with the Marx Brothers.

As we have seen, each of the Marxes has his own endearing characteristics. Each is a master of

his own brand of insanity. Together they are sheer comic dynamite. Their pictures all had portions that creaked and threatened to come apart at the seams, some more than others. But always, the brothers would bounce back with an inspired moment, and viewers dared not let their minds wander, for any of these moments might turn out to be one of their best routines.

There may be ambitious future funnymen who think that they can constitute a "second coming" of the Marx Brothers. Whatever they may accomplish on their own, the odds are solidly against their eclipsing Groucho, Chico and Harpo, whose films continue to rock audiences with laughter and reach across the years to successive generations.

The atomic age has given rise to speculation as to whether the world as we know it will survive. Certainly Marx Brothers films should be among the artifacts of our civilization that are preserved in a time capsule. Imagine explorers from other planets on an archaeological dig in the rubble that once was earth, just as our archaeologists have explored past civilizations. If they came across a preserved copy of *A Night at the Opera*, however little they knew about this epoch, they would most likely be in for some unexpected laughs. And perhaps, if they had learned enough to recognize and appreciate the satirical ingredients of *Duck Soup*, they might gain insight into why the earth people had obliterated each other. Chances are, wherever they might be from, that the power struggles of Freedonia and Sylvania might even remind them of home.

BIBLIOGRAPHY

Adamson, Joe. *Groucho, Harpo, Chico And Sometimes Zeppo.* Simon and Schuster, New York, 1973.

Agee, James. *Agee on Film.* Grosset & Dunlap, New York, 1969.

Anobile, Richard J. *Hooray For Captain Spaulding!* Darien House, Inc., New York, 1974.

Creelman, Eileen. "Picture Plays and Players: Chico, the Piano-playing Marx, Talks of 'Marx Bros. at the Circus.' " *New York Sun,* November 14, 1939.

Crichton, Kyle. *The Marx Brothers.* Doubleday & Company, Inc., New York, 1950.

"Day at The Races, A, or Facts about the Marxes." *New York Post,* June 12, 1937.

Day At The Races, A. The MGM Library of Film Scripts. The Viking Press, Inc., New York, 1972.

Dembart, Lee. "Groucho's 1950's Quiz Show is a hit all over again." *The New York Times,* March 9, 1975.

Esslin, Martin. *The Theatre of the Absurd.* Anchor Books, Doubleday & Company, Inc., New York, 1969.

Eyles, Allen. *The Marx Brothers: Their World of Comedy.* A. S. Barnes & Co., New York, 1974.

Four Marx Brothers, The, in Monkey Business and Duck Soup. Classic Film Scripts, Simon and Schuster, New York, 1972.

Greene, Laurence. "We're Through, Groucho Marx Says." *New York Post,* April 10, 1941.

Gussow, Mel. "Groucho Back in Town for 'Animal Crackers.' " *The New York Times,* June 21, 1974.

Hammond, Percy, "Zeppo Also Serves, Who Only Stands and Waits." *New York Herald Tribune,* clipping undated, c. October, 1928.

"Love Plots Aids Marx Laughs." (Interview with Sam Wood). *New York World-Telegram,* June 19, 1937.

Maltin, Leonard. *Movie Comedy Teams.* The New American Library, Inc., New York, 1974.

Marx, Arthur. *Life With Groucho.* Simon and Schuster, New York, 1954.

Marx, Arthur. *Son of Groucho.* David McKay Company, Inc., New York, 1972.

Marx, Groucho. *Groucho And Me.* Manor Books, Inc., New York, 1973.

Marx, Groucho. *The Groucho Letters.* Manor Books, Inc., New York, 1974.

Marx, Groucho and Richard J. Anobile. *The Marx Bros. Scrapbook*. Grosset & Dunlap, New York, 1974.

Marx, Harpo, with Rowland Barber. *Harpo Speaks!* Freeway Press, Inc., New York, 1974.

Meredith, Scott. *George S. Kaufman and His Friends*. Doubleday & Company, Inc., New York, 1974.

Morris, Mary, "News: Girl Chases Marx Brothers." *PM.*, New York, January 27, 1946.

New York Times Film Reviews, The. The New York Times & Arno Press, New York, 1970, 1971.

Night At The Opera, A. The MGM Library of Film Scripts. The Viking Press, Inc., New York, 1973.

Oppenheimer, George. "Forever Groucho." *Newsday*, Long Island, April 22, 1967.

Perelman, S. J. "The Winsome Foursome: How to go batty with the Marx Brothers when writing a film called 'Monkey Business.' " *Show*, November 1961.

Shabecoff, Philip. "A Belated Treat for Germans: Marx Brothers Movies on TV." *The New York Times*, February 13, 1967.

Woollcott, Alexander. "Harpo Marx and Some Brothers." *New York Sun*, May 20, 1924.

Woollcott, Alexander. *Obituary*. Shouts and Murmurs column, *The New Yorker*, September 28, 1929.

Zimmerman, Paul D., and Burt Goldblatt. *The Marx Brothers at The Movies*. G. P. Putnam's Sons, New York, 1968.

THE MAJOR FILMS OF
THE MARX BROTHERS

The director's name follows the release date. A (c) following the release date indicates that the film was in color. Sp indicates Screenplay and b/o indicates based/on.

1. THE COCOANUTS. Paramount, 1929. *Joseph Santley* and *Robert Florey*. Adapted by Morrie Ryskind, b/o musical comedy by George S. Kaufman; music and lyrics: Irving Berlin. Cast: Groucho, Harpo, Chico, Zeppo, Margaret Dumont, Mary Eaton, Oscar Shaw, Kay Francis, Cyril Ring, Basil Ruysdael. TEC

2. ANIMAL CRACKERS. Paramount, 1930. *Victor Heerman*. Sp: Morrie Ryskind, b/o musical comedy by George S. Kaufman and Morrie Ryskind; music and lyrics: Bert Kalmar, Harry Ruby. Cast: Groucho, Harpo, Chico, Zeppo, Margaret Dumont, Lillian Roth, Louis Sorin, Hal Thompson, Margaret Irving, Kathryn Reece, Robert Greig, Edward Metcalf.

3. MONKEY BUSINESS. Paramount, 1931. *Norman McLeod*. Sp: S. J. Perelman, Will B. Johnstone, with additional dialogue by Arthur Sheekman. Cast: Groucho, Harpo, Chico, Zeppo, Thelma Todd, Douglass Dumbrille, Rockcliffe Fellowes, Tom Kennedy, Ruth Hall, Harry Woods, Ben Taggart, Otto Fries, Evelyn Pierce, Maxine Castle.

4. HORSE FEATHERS. Paramount, 1932. *Norman McLeod*. Sp: Bert Kalmar, Harry Ruby, S. J. Perelman, and Will B. Johnstone; music and lyrics: Bert Kalmar and Harry Ruby. Cast: Groucho, Harpo, Chico, Zeppo, Thelma Todd, David Landau, Florine McKinney, James Pierce, Nat Pendleton, Reginald Barlow, Robert Greig, Ben Taggart.

5. DUCK SOUP. Paramount, 1933. *Leo McCarey*. Sp: Bert Kalmar and Harry Ruby; additional dialogue: Arthur Sheekman and Nat Perrin; music and lyrics: Bert Kalmar and Harry Ruby. Cast: Groucho, Harpo, Chico, Zeppo, Margaret Dumont, Raquel Torres, Louis Calhern, Verna Hillie, Leonid Kinsky, Edmund Breese, Edwin Maxwell.

BROWN - FREED "Alone"

KAPER - WASHINGTON "COSi COSA"

6. A NIGHT AT THE OPERA. MGM, 1935. *Sam Wood*. Sp: George S. Kaufman and Morrie Ryskind; additional material: Al Boasberg; b/o story by James Kevin McGuinness; music and lyrics: Nacio Herb Brown and Arthur Freed; Bronislau Kaper, Walter Jurmann, and Ned Washington. Cast: Groucho, Harpo, Chico, Margaret Dumont Siegfried Rumann, Kitty Carlisle, Allan Jones, Walter Woolf King, Edward Keane, Robert Emmett O'Connor, Billy Gilbert.

7. A DAY AT THE RACES. MGM, 1937. *Sam Wood*. Sp: Robert Pirosh, George Seaton, and George Oppenheimer, b/o story by Robert Pirosh and George Seaton; music and lyrics: Bronislau Kaper and Walter Jurmann, and Gus Kahn. Cast: Groucho, Harpo, Chico, Margaret Dumont, Siegfried Rumann, Allan Jones, Maureen O'Sullivan, Douglass Dumbrille, Leonard Ceeley, Esther Muir, Robert Middlemass, the Crinoline Choir, w| IVIE ANDERSON

8. ROOM SERVICE. RKO, 1938. *William A. Seiter*. Sp: Morrie Ryskind, b/o play by John Murray and Allen Boretz. Cast: Groucho, Harpo, Chico, Lucille Ball, Ann Miller, Frank Albertson, Donald MacBride, Cliff Dunstan, Philip Loeb, Philip Wood, Alexander Asro, Charles Halton.

9. AT THE CIRCUS. MGM, 1939. *Edward Buzzell*. Sp: Irving Brecher; music and lyrics: Harold Arlen and E. Y. Harburg. Cast: Groucho, Harpo, Chico, Margaret Dumont, Kenny Baker, Florence Rice, Eve Arden, Nat Pendleton, Fritz Feld, James Burke, Jerry Marenghi, Barnett Parker.

10. GO WEST. MGM, 1940. *Edward Buzzell*. Sp: Irving Brecher; music and lyrics: Bronislau Kaper, Gus Kahn, Roger Edens, Charles Wakefield Cadman. Cast: Groucho, Harpo, Chico, John Carroll, Diana Lewis, Walter Woolf King, Robert Barrat, June MacCloy, George Lessey.

11. THE BIG STORE. MGM, 1941. *Charles Riesner*. Sp: Sid Kuller, Hal Fimberg, Ray Golden, b/o story by Nat Perrin; music and lyrics. Hal Dorne, Sid Kuller, Ray Golden, Hal Fimberg, Ben Oakland, Artie Shaw, and Milton Drake. Cast: Groucho, Harpo, Chico, Margaret Dumont, Douglass Dumbrille, Tony Martin, Virginia Grey, William Tannen, Marion Martin, Virginia O'Brien, Henry Armetta, Anna Demetrio.

12. A NIGHT IN CASABLANCA. A David L. Loew Production, released by United Artists, 1946. *Archie Mayo*. Sp: Joseph Fields, Roland Kibbee; additional material: Frank Tashlin; music and lyrics: Ted Snyder, Bert Kalmar, and Harry Ruby. Cast: Groucho, Harpo, Chico, Siegfried Rumann, Lisette Verea, Charles Drake, Lois Collier, Dan Seymour, Lewis Russell, Harro Mellor, Frederick Gierman.

13. LOVE HAPPY. A Lester Cowan Production, released by United Artists, 1949. *David Miller*. Sp: Frank Tashlin and Mac Benoff, b/o story by Harpo Marx. Cast: Groucho, Harpo, Chico, Ilona Massey, Vera-Ellen, Marion Hutton, Raymond Burr, Bruce Gordon, Melville Cooper, Leon Belasco, Paul Valentine, Eric Blore, Marilyn Monroe.

MISCELLANY

TOO MANY KISSES. Paramount, 1925. *Paul Sloane.* b/o story "A Maker of Gestures" by John Monk Saunders. Harpo in supporting role in cast headed by Richard Dix, William Powell, and Frances Howard.

HUMORISK. c. 1926. Made privately by the Marx Brothers and never released. Presumed destroyed.

HOLLYWOOD ON PARADE. Paramount, 1932. Short. Off-screen footage of Groucho, Harpo, and Chico with their families; also Skeets Gallagher, Fifi D'Orsay, Eddie Lambert and his Orchestra, and others.

HOLLYWOOD ON PARADE. Paramount, 1933. Short. Cast: Chico, Buster Crabbe, W. C. Fields, Earl Carroll Girls.

LA FIESTA DE SANTA BARBARA. MGM, 1935 (c). Short. Cast: Harpo, Buster Keaton, Leo Carrillo, Robert Taylor, Judy Garland (Frances Gumm), Gary Cooper, Ida Lupino.

THE KING AND THE CHORUS GIRL. Warner Brothers, 1937. *Mervyn LeRoy.* Sp: Norman Krasna and Groucho Marx; music and lyrics: Walter H. Heymann and Ted Koehler. Cast: Fernand Gravet, Joan Blondell, Edward Everett Horton, Alan Mowbray, Jane Wyman.

SCREEN SNAPSHOTS NO. 2. Columbia, 1943. *Ralph Staub.* Short. Groucho does a radio broadcast with Carole Landis. Footage repeated in Snapshot entry HOLLYWOOD'S GREAT COMEDIANS, 1953.

SCREEN SNAPSHOTS NO. 8. Columbia, 1943. *Ralph Staub.* Short. Groucho, Harpo, Chico with the Ritz Brothers, Gene Autry, Tyrone Power, Annabella, Kay Kyser, Alan Mowbray, Lou Holtz.

STAGE DOOR CANTEEN. A Sol Lesser Production, released by United Artists, 1943. *Frank Borzage.* Sp: Delmer Daves. Harpo among all-star guests, including Tallulah Bankhead, Katharine Cornell, Katharine Hepburn, Alfred Lunt, Lynn Fontanne, Helen Hayes, Ethel Merman, Paul Muni.

ALL-STAR BOND RALLY. Twentieth Century-Fox, 1945. *Michael Audley.* Short. Harpo with Bob Hope, Bing Crosby, Fibber McGee and Molly, Frank Sinatra, Harry James' Band, Betty Grable, Jeanne Crain, Linda Darnell, Faye Marlowe, Carmen Miranda.

COPACABANA. A Sam Coslow Production, released by United Artists, 1947. *Alfred E. Green.* Sp: Laslo Vadnay, Allen Boretz, and Howard Harris, b/o story by Laslo Vadnay. Cast: Groucho, Carmen Miranda, Andy Russell, Steve Cochran, Gloria Jean, Ralph Sanford, Louis Sobol, Earl Wilson, Abel Green.

MR. MUSIC. Paramount, 1950. *Richard Haydn.* Sp: Arthur Sheekman, b/o play *Accent On Youth* by Samson Raphaelson. Cast: Bing Crosby, Nancy Olson, Charles Coburn, Ruth Hussey, Robert Stack, Marge and Gower Champion. Groucho makes guest appearance and performs skit based on song *Life Is So Peculiar.*

DOUBLE DYNAMITE. RKO, 1951. *Irving Cummings.* Sp: Melville Shavelson, b/o story by Leo Rosten. Cast: Groucho, Frank Sinatra, Jane Russell, Don McGuire, Howard Freeman.

A GIRL IN EVERY PORT. RKO, 1952. *Chester Erskine.* Sp: Chester Erskine, b/o story by Frederick Hazlitt Brennan. Cast: Groucho, Marie Wilson, William Bendix, Don DeFore, Gene Lockhart.

WILL SUCCESS SPOIL ROCK HUNTER. Twentieth Century-Fox, 1957 (c). *Frank Tashlin.* Sp: Frank Tashlin, b/o play by George Axelrod. Cast: Jayne Mansfield, Tony Randall, Joan Blondell, Mickey Hargitay. Groucho appears very briefly at the end.

THE STORY OF MANKIND. Warner Brothers, 1957 (c). *Irwin Allen.* Sp: Irwin Allen and Charles Bennett, b/o book by Hendrik Willem van Loon. Cast of "name" actors, including Ronald Colman, Hedy Lamarr, Virginia Mayo, Agnes Moorehead, Vincent Price, Cedric Hardwicke, with Groucho as Peter Minuit, Harpo as Isaac Newton, Chico as a monk, Groucho's wife Eden Hartford as Laughing Water, Groucho's daughter Melinda as an Early Christian Child.

SHOWDOWN AT ULCER GULCH. Shamus-Culhane Productions, 1958. Commercial short for *The Saturday Evening Post.* Groucho and Chico with Ernie Kovacs, Edie Adams, Bob Hope, Bing Crosby, Salome Jens, Orson Bean.

SKIDOO. Paramount, 1968 (c). *Otto Preminger.* Sp: Doran William Cannon. Cast: Jackie Gleason, Carol Channing, Frankie Avalon, Fred Clark, Peter Lawford, Burgess Meredith, George Raft. Groucho appears briefly as "God," the head of a criminal syndicate.

INDEX

Abbott, George, 96
Adams, Franklin P., 36, 37
Agee, James, 112, 116
Albee, E. F., 34
Allen, Irwin, 121
Allen, Woody, 141
Anderson, Ivy, 92
Animal Crackers, 12, 14, 23, 40-51, 58
Animal Crackers (stage), 37, 38, 39, 43, 44, 47, 48
Anobile, Richard, 25
Arden, Eve, 101, 103
Arlen, Harold, 101
At the Circus, 100-103, 105, 106

Baker, Kenny, 101
Ball, Lucille, 96
Bankhead, Tallulah, 37
Benchley, Robert, 37
Bendix, William, 122
Benny, Jack, 33
Berlin, Irving, 37
Bernhardt, Sarah, 33
"Best of Groucho, The", 126
Big Store, The, 95, 106, 109-110
Blazing Saddles, 141
Blondell, Joan, 126
Boasberg, Al, 78, 79, 85
Boehnel, William, 103
Bogart, Humphrey, 110
Brecher, Irving, 101, 103
Broody, Herman, 36
Brooks, Mel, 141
Broun, Heywood, 37
Buzzell, Edward, 101, 103

Calhern, Louis, 71
Capone, Al, 33
Carlisle, Kitty, 79, 81
Casablanca, 110
Ceeley, Leonard, 87

Chaplin, Charles, 12, 33, 58, 112, 136
Chevalier, Maurice, 56
Citizen Kane, 54
Cocoanuts, The, 39, 42-47, 48, 53, 54
Cocoanuts, The (stage), 37, 43, 44
Cohen, John S., Jr., 75
Connelly, Marc, 37
Copacabana, 116
Creelman, Eileen, 96
Crosby, Bing, 122
Crowther, Bosley, 116
Davis, Mildred, 39
Day at the Races, A, 75, 85-94, 95, 136
Dix, Richard, 39
Double Dynamite, 122
Duck Soup, 64, 67, 71-76, 77, 95, 144
Dumbrille, Douglass, 90, 109
Dumont, Margaret, 11, 44, 46, 48, 50, 56, 71, 79, 81, 87, 87, 101, 103, 104, 136

Eaton, Mary, 42
Edwards, Gus, 30

Favre-Le Bret, Robert, 11
Fields, Joseph, 112
Fields, W. C., 136
Fifth Season, The, 126
Fimberg, Hal, 106
Fisher, Art, 32
Fleming, Erin, 11, 12
Florey, Robert, 42, 43, 46
Francis, Kay, 44
Fratillini Brothers, the, 36

Gable, Clark, 130
General, The, 105
Girl in Every Port, A, 122
Go West, 103-106
Gold Rush, The, 58
Golden, Ray, 106
Gravet, Fernand, 126

Great Jewel Robbery, The, 122
Grey, Virginia, 109
Guss, Harry L., 81

Hall, Mordaunt, 47, 53, 58, 64, 75
Hammond, Percy, 37, 44
Harburg, E. Y., 101
Hardy, Oliver, 71, 141
Harpo Speaks!, 15
Harris, Sam, 37, 71
Hart, Teddy, 96
Heerman, Victor, 48
Horse Feathers, 30, 58-64, 75
Horton, Edward Everett, 126
Humorisk, 39

I'll Say She Is, 36-37
Ionesco, Eugene, 132

Jackson, Joe, 36
Johnstone, Will B., 54, 55, 58
Jones, Allan, 79, 81, 90

Kalmar, Bert, 37, 48, 58, 62, 71, 78, 86
Kaufman, Beatrice, 37
Kaufman, George S., 37, 38, 53, 78, 79, 85
Keaton, Buster, 12, 105, 136
Kennedy, Edgar, 71
Kibbee, Roland, 112
King and the Chorus Girl, The, 126
Krasna, Norman, 126
Kuller, Sid, 106

Lardner, Ring, 37
Lasky, Jesse, 54
Laurel, Stan, 71, 141
LeRoy, Mervyn, 101

Levene, Sam, 96
Lewis, Jerry, 141
Lloyd, Harold, 136
Loew, David L., 116
Lollobrigida, Gina, 12
Lombard, Carole, 130
Love Happy, 116, 120

MacMurray, Fred, 130
McCarey, Leo, 67, 71
McGuinness, James Kevin, 78
McLeod, Norman Z., 55, 58
Mankiewicz, Herman, 37, 54, 55, 58
Martin, Dean, 141
Martin, Tony, 109
Marx, Arthur, 29, 103, 126, 131
Marx Bros. Scrapbook, The, 25
Marx, Gummo, 15, 16, 23, 25, 27, 30, 32, 33, 130, 131
Marx, Minnie, 15, 16, 18, 19, 23, 25, 26, 29, 32, 34, 36, 47
Marx, Sam ("Frenchie"), 16, 18, 23, 58n
Massey, Ilona, 120
Melrose, Bert, 36
Miller, Alice Duer, 37
Miller, Ann, 96
Minnie's Boys, 126
Miranda, Carmen, 116
Monkey Business, 54-58
Monroe, Marilyn, 120n
Morris, Mary, 76
Mowbray, Alan, 126
Mr. Music, 122
Muir, Esther, 90

Nathan, George Jean, 37
Night at the Opera, A, 11. 75, 78-85, 95n 144
Night in Casablanca, A, 110, 112, 116

Nugent, Frank S., 100, 103

O'Brien, Virginia, 109
Oppenheimer, George, 85
O'Sullivan, Maureen, 90

Parker, Dorothy, 37
Pelswick, Rose, 100
Pendleton, Nat, 62, 101
Perelman, S. J., 54, 55, 58
Perrin, Nat, 54, 55, 71, 106
Pirosh, Robert, 85
Pryor, Thomas M., 106, 120
Pusey, J. Carver, 54

Rice, Florence, 101
Riesner, Charles, 106
Ritz Brothers, The, 141
Room Service, 18, 95, 96-100, 101
Ross, Harold, 37
Roth, Lillian, 48
Ruby, Harry, 37, 48, 58, 62, 71, 78, 86
Rumann, Siegfried, 79, 81, 90, 112
Russell, Andy, 116
Russell, Jane, 122
Ryskind, Morrie, 37, 43, 48, 78, 79, 96

Santley, Joseph, 42
Scenes from A Night at the Opera, 79
Scheuer, Philip K., 64, 75
Schoenberg, Fanny, 16
Schoenberg, Lafe, 16
Seaton, George, 85
Seiter, William A., 96
Sennett, Mack, 48
Sennwald, Andre, 84
Shaw, Oscar, 42
Shean, Al, 15, 25, 26, 30, 32

Shean, Lou, 27
Sheekman, Arthur, 54, 55, 71
Sherwood, Robert, 37
Sinatra, Frank, 122
Son of Groucho, 29, 126
Stage Door Canteen, 110
Stanwyck, Barbara, 130
Stewart, Donald Ogden, 37
Story of Mankind, The, 121
Strauss, Theodore, 109

Tashlin, Frank, 112
Taylor, Deems, 37
Taylor, Robert, 130
Thalberg, Irving, 77, 78, 79, 81, 85, 95, 100
Three Stooges, the, 141
Time for Elizabeth, 126
Todd, Thelma, 56, 58, 62
Too Many Kisses, 39
Towering Inferno, The, 121

van Loon, Hendrik Willem, 121
Verea, Lisette, 112

Wanger, Walter, 42
Warner, Harry, 112
Warner, Jack, 112
Watts, Richard, Jr., 75
Wilson, Marie, 122
Winchell, Walter, 38
Winsten, Archer, 96
Wood, Sam, 78, 79, 94
Woollcott, Alexander, 15, 36, 37, 38, 132
Wyman, Jane, 126

"You Bet Your Life", 124

Zunser, Jesse, 100, 103

ABOUT THE AUTHOR
William Wolf has been film critic for *Cue* Magazine since 1964 and is a former chairman of the New York Film Critics. He teaches "Film as Literature" in the English Department at New York University and "Contemporary Cinema" in the Communications Arts Department of St. John's University. His articles on the arts appear in major American newspapers, and are internationally syndicated. The author, who grew up in Bound Brook, New Jersey, and is a graduate of Rutgers University, lives in New York City. He is married and is the father of two daughters.

ABOUT THE EDITOR
Ted Sennett is the author of *Warner Brothers Presents*, a tribute to the great Warners films of the Thirties and Forties, and of *Lunatics and Lovers*, on the long-vanished but well-remembered "screwball" comedies of the past. He is also the editor of *The Movie Buff's Book* and has written about films for magazines and newspapers. He lives in New Jersey with his wife and three children.